# Life Science 1

## *The Activities*
## *of*
## *Life*

## PATHWAYS IN SCIENCE

# PATHWAYS

# IN SCIENCE

## Life Science 1

# *The Activities of Life*

## Joseph M. Oxenhorn

### Edited by Peter Greenleaf

**Consultants:**

**John Donahue**
*Science Consultant*
*Archdiocese of Chicago*

**Neal Eigenfeld**
*Curriculum Specialist, Science Education*
*Milwaukee Public Schools*

**Susan F. MacGill**
*Science Department Chairperson*
*Pinellas County School System*
*Clearwater, Florida*

**Myrna Stoflet**
*Science Teacher*
*John O'Connell School of Technology*
*San Francisco UFSD*

**Globe Book Company**
New York / Chicago / Cleveland

AUTHOR/Joseph M. Oxenhorn has been a teacher and Department Head of science in various secondary schools and has served as principal of elementary, junior, and senior high schools. He has been active in science syllabus preparation and has trained science teachers. Since his retirement from his post as principal of Theodore Roosevelt High School, he has served as senior science author for Globe Book Company. He is the author of *Pathways in Biology, Oceanography and Our Future, Energy and Our Future,* and a book for teachers on methods of teaching science.

EDITOR/Peter Greenleaf served as chairman of the science department in various secondary schools. He was Supervisor of Audio-Visual Instruction (science specialist) for the New York City Board of Education. He has headed science syllabus committees and has trained science teachers. He is the author of many science books and numerous related articles, films, and filmstrips. He is coauthor of Globe's *Pathways—Insights into Science* and *Experiences in Science.* He was an instructor of Physics at the Cooper Union College of Engineering. He was Adjunct Associate Professor of Physics and Astronomy at Brooklyn College and at St. John's University, Staten Island.

Ruth G. Oxenhorn served as Editorial and Research Assistant in the original and revised editions.

Art by Ayres Houghtelling, Ted Burwell, Mel Erickson, Dyno Lowenstein Pictograph Corp., Studio 43, P.I.P.
Text and Cover Design by Bill Gray
Photo Editor: Adelaide Garvin Ungerland

**Photo Acknowledgments**

The photographs included in this text, on the pages indicated below, appear courtesy of the following:

American Cyanimid Company, Lederle Laboratories Division: 168. American Museum of Natural History: 8 (right), 12. American Optometric Association: 152. American Red Cross of Greater New York: 133. Bausch and Lomb: 107. California Academy of Sciences: 8 (left), 91. Carolina Biological Supply Company: 13, 72, 92 (left and right), 93, 108 (upper), 144. Dr. E.R. Degginger/Bruce Coleman: 148. M.L.P. Fogden/Bruce Coleman: 6, 25 (right). Dr. E.R. Degginger: 28. From *Tissues and Organs: A Text Atlas of Scanning Electron Microscopy* by Richard G. Kessel and Randy H. Kardon. W.A. Freeman and Company. © 1979: 108 (lower), 156. German Information Center: 170. Beryl Goldberg © 1979: 7, 43, 49, 71, 86. Burton Goldfield: 14(right). Jain Kelly: 40. Arthur Mina: 25 (left). National Film Board of Canada: 78 (lower). N.A.S.A.: 16. Joseph M. Oxenhorn: 14 (left), 78 (upper), 88, 163. Chas. Pfizer, Inc.: 38. H. Armstrong Roberts: 2, 34, 56, 142. Sargent-Welch Scientific Company: 19, 30. Secondary School Project, Princeton University: 48. Alfred Owczarzak/Taurus Photos: 98. Irv Savlowitz/Taurus Photos: 145. Dave Woodward/Taurus Photos: 166 (upper). Samuel Teicher: 5, 101, 162. United Press International: 130, 166 (lower). U.S.D.A.: 39.

ISBN 0-87065-688-0 Softcover    ISBN 0-87065-663-5 Hardcover
Printed in the United States of America  1  2  3  4  5  6  7  8  9  0

# Contents

# *List of Investigations*

# Introduction to the Students

Welcome to your new science book, *Pathways in Science!*

A pathway is a road, a street, or an avenue which leads you somewhere. *Pathways in Science* is a book that will lead you to a greater understanding of science.

This section of *Pathways* is called *The Activities of Life*. It is Book 1 of *Life Science*. In this section, you will be studying a branch of science called *biology*. Biology is the study of living things: what they look like, how they work, and what they do. It is an exciting science and will answer many questions for you.

*Pathways* is a tool to help you learn. Good mechanics know their tools. A good student knows how to use the book.

Let us study the organization of the book and see how to use it.

## Arrangement

At the front of the book is a *Table of Contents*. This table, or list, tells you what you can find in the book. It tells you on what page each part of the book can be found.

The book is divided into five parts called *Units.*

Each unit is divided into *Chapters*. Each chapter begins with a *Target Question* which is answered by material in that chapter. For example, on page 4, you will find Chapter 1. The target question is, "How do we use our senses to learn about plants and animals?"

Each chapter is divided into *Sections* which have a number. Turn to page 4. There you will find Section 1, *Stop . . . Look . . . Learn*. Section 2 on the same page is titled *Living things are everywhere*.

Every few sections you will find a "break" called *Learned So Far*. Turn to page 6 for an example. This is a summary of what you have just read. It helps you review. It helps you remember.

At the end of each chapter, you will find questions which test how much you have learned. Turn to page 31.

There you will find the section called *Self-Study Guide for Chapter 4*.

In addition to the questions, you will also find suggestions for exciting things you can do at home. *Do and Discover* experiments are exciting amateur science investigations. In the *Looking Further* exercises, there are suggestions of interesting places to visit where you will learn about science.

### New Science Words

Science has its own language. It has new words which have special meanings. Some of these new words might look strange to you. The book tells you how to pronounce these words. Turn to page 4. In Section 2, we use the word BIOLOGIST. Notice how it is pronounced: (by-OL-uh-jist).

At the end of the book there is a *Glossary*. Turn to page 174. Notice that the words are arranged in alphabetical order. In column two, the words are written as they are pronounced. In column three, there are simple definitions.

### Pictures and Diagrams

The book has many pictures and diagrams to help you "see" science ideas. All pictures and diagrams are numbered in such a way that you can find them quickly. For example, 45–1 means the first picture on page 45; 69–2 means the second picture on page 69.

### Marginal Notes

The *Marginal Notes* throughout the book contain many useful and interesting science ideas.

### Investigations

Pathways has many *Investigations*. Some of them you will see your teacher do in class. Some you will do in class by yourself or with a partner. Some you can do at home. Investigations are great fun and a good way to learn. The list of investigations appears on page vi.

### Read All About It

Reading is one of the most important ways to learn.

1.  Visit your school and/or local library. Find out where the science books are shelved.
2.  Look up facts in an encyclopedia, in an almanac, and in the Reader's Guide to Periodical Literature.
3.  Your librarian can help you.

# It's fun to study living things

## Unit I/outline

# It's fun to study living things

## What's it all about?

It's fun. . . . It's knowledge. . . . It's practical and useful. Life science, or BIOLOGY (by-OL-uh-jee), is one of the branches of science. In the study of life science we look for questions about living things and try to find the answers.

Life science is for everyone. You can receive the benefits from the discoveries made by life scientists. Life science even enters into what you do for a hobby or to have fun.

We have seen that a life may be saved by transplanting a healthy kidney in place of a diseased one. We have seen our farms producing more and more food for a growing and hungry world. But will we find a cure for cancer or diabetes? Can we clean our polluted waters so that seafood may be eaten safely? Can growing more trees for fuel help us solve the energy crisis?

You have probably enjoyed a Sunday in the park as you watched birds. Or perhaps you have hiked through the woods and noticed the spring flowers or the tall trees reaching for the sky. Our lives are made richer by the beauty of the living things that surround us.

In this unit you will learn
- some of the "signs of life."
- how your senses help you study life.
- where people study living things.
- how living things are related to their environment.

*And just as important,* you will learn
- how you can study living things at home.
- how you can develop new hobbies in life science.

## chapter 1

**TARGET** How do we use our senses to learn about plants and animals?

# Watching plants and animals at work

Fig. 4-1

4

## 1-1. Stop . . . look . . . learn

A familiar sign at railroad crossings reads: STOP! LOOK! LISTEN! This is *almost* the way scientists work. But they might change the sign to read: STOP! LOOK! LEARN! Much of what scientists know about living plants and animals was learned by doing just that.

Curious people, like scientists, patiently plan how to find out about things. Then they look very carefully to be sure their information is right. As a result they learn a great deal.

## 1-2. Living things are everywhere

Have you ever been to summer camp? If so, you have probably been on a "nature walk." You may have gone for a walk in the woods or to a pond or up a mountain.

Scientists may also go on nature walks to learn about living things. A scientist who studies living things is called a BIOLOGIST (by-OL-uh-jist). A NATURALIST (NACH-ruh-list) is a biologist who studies nature. A naturalist may walk in the woods, study wild animals in the jungle, or take a boat to a faraway island. Some have camped in the desert. Others have gone to the bottom of the ocean. A new way that scientists have found to gather facts has been to fly in space and walk on the moon.

But do *you* have to travel great distances to learn about living things? Of course not! You can watch birds on a telephone line. You can observe (watch) flies on a ceiling and animals in a zoo. Living things are everywhere. How can we study them?

## 1-3. Looking more carefully

About two thousand years ago, in far-off ancient Greece, there lived a wise man named ARISTOTLE (AR-ih-STOT-ul). He was curious about many things. One of the things that interested him was how an egg develops into a chicken.

Like many other people, he observed how a mother hen sits on an egg and warms it until it hatches. But Aristotle did more. He took an egg from a mother hen the day she began sitting on it, broke it open and looked at it very carefully. He made a drawing of what he saw. Then he took a second egg from a mother hen after she sat on it for two days. Again, he broke the egg open, observed it carefully and drew a diagram. He did the same with a three-day egg, a four-day egg and so on for 21 days. That's how long it takes for a chicken egg to hatch. Then Aristotle had the complete story. He was so careful in his work that in two thousand years only a few small errors have been found in his observations (ob-zur-VAY-shunz).

**Fig. 5-1**

An incubator keeps a steady temperature for hatching eggs. How would use of an incubator aid observation?

**Fig. 6-1**

This giant redwood started as a tiny seed and may grow to over 100 meters tall. What can you learn about its growth by observation?

### Learned So Far . . .

- Seeing is observing.
- By observing, we learn about living things, their activities and their needs.
- Naturalists and biologists study life.

### 1-4. How do living things grow?

By observing carefully, Aristotle was able to learn how an egg grows to be a chicken. By observation *you* can learn how a chick sheds its young soft feathers (*down*) and grows to be a mature hen or rooster with bigger and tougher feathers. You can learn how babies grow to be adults, or how a flower bud opens into a full flower. In other words, by observation, you can learn about *growth*. All living things, or ORGANISMS (OR-guh-niz-umz), grow.

### 1-5. How are living things built?

If you watch a fly, you will see that it has six legs. In the same way, you can discover that a spider has eight legs and that a worm has none. The feathers of a parakeet's *wings* are soft, but the *tail* feathers are stiff.

**Fig. 6-2**

Make observations about structure and behavior from these pictures.

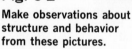

Using a mirror, look into your mouth. Observe the different shapes of your teeth. Now look into your eyes. See how the color near the black spot in each eye is different from the color at the edges? By observation you can learn about the *parts* of plants and animals—their STRUCTURE (STRUK-chur).

### 1-6. How can we observe living things at work?

MAURICE MAETERLINCK (MAY-tur-link) was a famous writer and lawyer who was interested in bees. For over 20 years, Maeterlinck watched bees in their beehives. He saw how the queen bee was cared for and how the "worker" bees made honey. He kept careful notes and wrote a wonderful book called *The Life of the Bee*. If you have a cat, hamster, or dog, you can observe your pet's habits. How does it eat, sleep, run, fight, and play? You can watch an insect on a summer night fly around and around an electric light. You can see that a plant's leaves turn brown when it doesn't get water. In each example, you are observing all the things that plants and animals do or, in other words, their BEHAVIOR (bih-HAY-vyur).

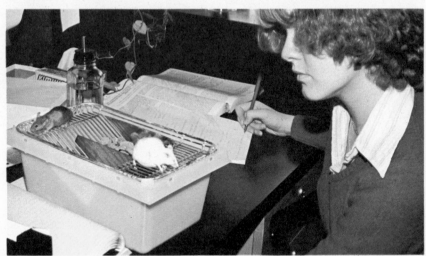

**Fig. 7-1**
The student of life science and hobbyist care for living things and make careful observations.

### Learned So Far . . .

- Observation helps us learn about the STRUCTURE, GROWTH, and BEHAVIOR of living things.
- Observation needs our patience, time, and care.

### 1-7. Your fingers can tell you

So far we have used the word *observation* to mean only "seeing with our eyes." But, of course, we can also learn with our other senses. Have you ever grabbed a rose bush? If you have, your *sense of touch* probably told you about the sharp *thorns*. Have you ever been stung by a jellyfish while you were swimming in the ocean? Your sense of touch probably told you to move away fast. It's easy to tell, even with your eyes closed, that a leaf from a tree is smoother than its bark. The fur of a collie is softer than that of a wire-haired terrier.

**Fig. 8-1**

Which sense other than seeing will teach you the difference between these two animals?

### 1-8. Your nose can tell you

You can also use your *sense of smell* to learn about living things. Flowers are beautiful to look at. Many also have a pleasant odor that helps you recognize them. Pine woods are easy to recognize even if your eyes are closed. Books about plants often describe them by their odor. The odor of a skunk is not easy to forget!

Carbon monoxide and carbon dioxide are two odorless gases found in the air. Which is the dangerous one?

### 1-9. Taste to learn

Scientists also identify living things by *taste*—another one of our five senses. We speak of sweet strawberries, salty fish, sour grapes, and bitter almonds. Wild animals learn quickly not to bite into certain plants because of their bitter or sour tastes.

### 1-10. Listen to learn

A dog's bark, a cat's meow, and a bird's song are probably very familiar to you. In the quiet of the country, you can hear the crickets chirping and the robins warbling. By listening to your heart, the doctor can tell you about your health. Yes, *hearing* also helps you learn.

**Fig. 9-1**

Put water in two jars. Add salt to one. Ask another student to identify the jar with salt. Which sense will they need to use to answer the question?

### Learned So Far . . .

- We can study living things by observation with our five senses: seeing, hearing, touching, tasting, and smelling.

---

## SELF-STUDY GUIDE FOR CHAPTER 1

All answers should be written in your notebook. Please do not write in this book.

### Understanding the reading

A. *Find the Answers*
Write the letter of the correct answer.
1. What is the main idea of Chapter 1?
    a. Observing plants and animals may teach us how they carry on their life activities.
    b. Without Aristotle's observations, we never would have understood how chicks hatch from eggs.
    c. Observation needs our time and patience.
    d. Naturalists are animal watchers.
2. When you examine the parts of a dog's paw, you are studying
    a. structure.
    b. behavior.
    c. growth.
    d. organisms.
3. Which may have been one of Aristotle's observations?

a. All eggs take 21 days to hatch.
b. Hens are covered with down.
c. Certain chicken feed makes the eggs white.
d. Mother hens warm their eggs.
4. A good example of the behavior of a bird is its
    a. size.
    b. color.
    c. feathers.
    d. flying habits.
5. Maeterlinck observed
    a. the migration of bees.
    b. how a queen bee is cared for.
    c. how bees protect themselves from bats.
    d. that bees differ from porcupines.

B. *True or False*
If the statement is true, write *true*. If the

statement is false, change the word in *italics* to make the statement true.

1. The scales of a fish are an example of its *behavior*.
2. *Naturalists* study living things.
3. Aristotle kept a record of his *observations*.
4. By observing that leaves are green we use our sense of *hearing*.

C. *Locate the Idea*
Find the section in which each of these questions is answered. Write the number of the section and one or two sentences that answer the question.

1. How are the feathers in the same bird different from one another?
2. Where do naturalists go to study living things?
3. How did Aristotle record his observations?
4. How could you tell you were in a pine forest even with your eyes closed?

## Word tools

Find the correct definition from *Column B* which describes the word in *Column A*. (One definition will not be used.)

**Column A**

1. naturalist
2. behavior
3. observation
4. down
5. structure

**Column B**

a. the activities of living things
b. information we get from seeing, touching, tasting, smelling, or hearing
c. a student of plants and animals
d. the parts of living things
e. soft feathers of a bird
f. an animal's ability to see

## Knowing what and why

A. *Understanding the Pictures*
1. Look back to Figure 8-1. Make two columns, one for the rabbit and one for the porcupine. In each column write three words that describe the appearance of these animals. Can you describe the texture of each of these animals by the picture?
2. Look back to Figure 6-1. Write four statements that you can make about the redwood tree. Can you write an observation about its size? Why or why not?

B. *Puzzling It Out*
Answer these questions in a sentence or two.
1. How might Aristotle's observations be different today?
2. How would you describe a rose to a person who cannot see?

## Looking further

1. Visit a local pet shop, zoo, or aquarium. Observe two of the animals. Describe their structure and behavior. How are the two animals alike? How are they different?
2. Choose an animal or plant that is familiar to you. Describe it to friends and see how many words it takes you until they guess your plant or animal.

## chapter 2

**TARGET**     **Where do scientists study living things?**

# *The world is so full of living things*

### 2-1. Looking back. . .

We can learn a great deal about living things without travel-ing far from home. We can study life in our own surroundings or ENVIRONMENT (en-VY-run-munt). We can look in parks, on nearby farms, and even in our own homes. But there are different kinds of living things in other places. Often we must go "into the field"—sometimes to faraway places to see the variety of living things.

### 2-2. Biologists are explorers

Off they go! By ship, by plane, by train, and on foot! Biolo-gists may have to be explorers in far-off places. Where do they go?

They carry their packs with cameras and collecting jars. They haul cages and field glasses. They bring MICRO-SCOPES (MY-kruh-skohps) and notebooks.

Biologists are explorers. Biologists are also scientists. Most of all, they are people who bring their curiosity and their desire to know wherever they travel.

### 2-3. A man . . . a ship . . . and an idea

Let us take an example—the English biologist, CHARLES

DARWIN. In 1831 he sailed on a ship called the *Beagle*. He visited faraway lands and the GALÁPAGOS (guh-LA-puh-gohs) Islands off the shores of Ecuador in South America.

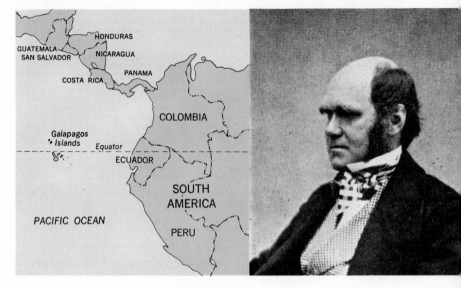

**Fig. 12-1**

Charles Darwin explored the natural world for years. He studied life near the equator. What natural living things can you study where you live?

He returned to England in 1836—five years later. He brought back with him many notebooks filled with observations about birds, insects, coral, tortoises (turtles), and fish. He also brought back a large nature collection as well as many new ideas about living things.

### 2-4. To Lapland on foot

Another famous journey was that of CAROLUS LINNAEUS (lih-NEE-us), a Swedish naturalist. In 1729 Linnaeus began exploring Lapland in the Far North. He made most of this journey on foot, making observations, collecting samples, and making drawings. As a result of his explorations, he developed a system for naming plants and animals. His system for naming different kinds or SPECIES (SPEE-sheez) of organisms is still used today.

### Learned So Far . . .

● Biologists sometimes go to faraway places to study living things.

**Fig. 13-1**
What observations can you make about this animal? What does it look like? What does it eat?

### 2-5. A walk in the woods

A walk in the woods will give you a chance to see many living things. You will see tall pine trees, trailing berry bushes, and scampering chipmunks. You will catch the flash of red on a bird's wing. Turn over a log and you will see bugs hurry out of sight. You may be frightened by the rapid movement of a garter snake or the whine of a green fly. A beautiful giant butterfly may stop one inch from you and disappear in a second when you try to catch it.

Naturalists often collect samples to bring home to study. A nature collection of insects and leaves can be the beginning of a wonderful hobby.

### 2-6. At the seashore

Walk along an ocean beach some day. You will see all kinds of living things that come from the sea. The beach probably has many shells that once held living oysters and clams. If you dig below the wet sand, you may be lucky enough to find some live shelled creatures—a mussel or clam or a little sea crab. You can learn to identify their shells very quickly.

### 2-7. On the ocean . . . in the ocean

Fishing can be a great sport—especially if you eat what you catch! But "going fishing" can also mean learning. Many scientists have spent hours on boats, catching fish to study and dissect. Perhaps you yourself have gone crabbing. When you raise the crab basket, you have a chance to study the structure and behavior of crabs.

**Fig. 14-1**

William Beebe developed this bathysphere used by deep-sea divers. In the picture on the right, navy deep-sea divers bring back information about life under the ocean's surface.

Studying fish and other kinds of animals under the ocean has become very easy with modern diving equipment. One of the most fascinating adventures has been in a BATHY-SCAPHE (BATH-ih-skayf), a kind of submarine that can travel to the ocean floor. From inside a bathyscaphe scientists can use special cameras to take pictures of ocean creatures.

### 2-8. A trip in the desert

The word *desert* probably brings to your mind a great deal of sand, very little water and not much life. But biologists have explored deserts and have found living things of great interest, such as desert plants, cactus, and lizards. There are many scientists who go to deserts on "digs." By excavating (digging) in sand, they sometimes find bones and fossils of animals that lived very long ago.

### 2-9. A walk on the moon

On July 20, 1969, the U.S. astronaut NEIL ARMSTRONG became the first man to walk on the moon. When the space program was first being developed, many questions were raised: Can humans live in space? What would the gravity of the moon (only 1/6 of earth's gravity) do to the human body? Would a person's eyesight, blood system, and nerves be able to work properly?

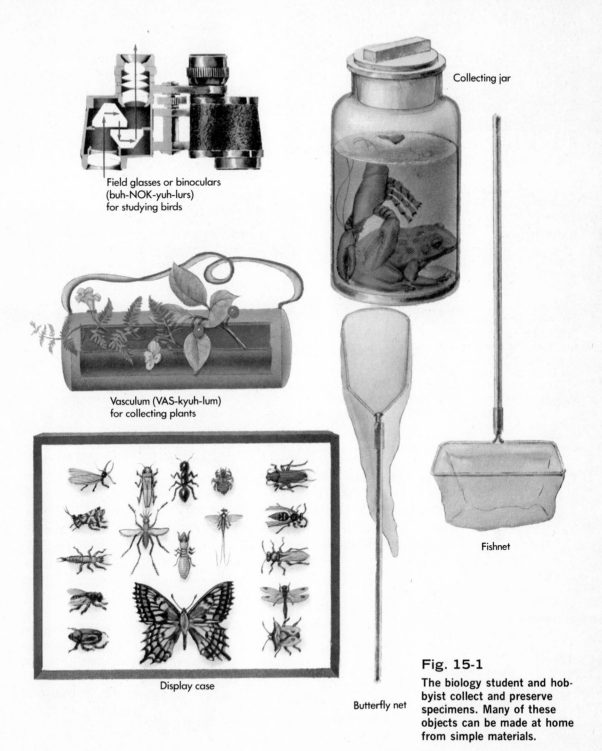

Field glasses or binoculars
(buh-NOK-yuh-lurs)
for studying birds

Collecting jar

Vasculum (VAS-kyuh-lum)
for collecting plants

Fishnet

Display case

Butterfly net

**Fig. 15-1**

The biology student and hobbyist collect and preserve specimens. Many of these objects can be made at home from simple materials.

Some of these questions were answered in the laboratory. But, it was impossible to answer all of the questions without actually going to the moon. To help the astronauts survive on the moon, a special space suit was developed. It created a familiar environment for their bodies with air pressure and temperature like that on Earth.

**Fig. 16-1**

ASTRONAUTS (AS-truh-nots) brought back information about how human beings react to being in space and on the moon.

## Learned So Far . . .

● Living things are studied in the woods, near oceans, in the desert, and even in space.

## SELF-STUDY GUIDE FOR CHAPTER 2

All answers should be written in your notebook. Please do not write in this book.

### Understanding the reading

A. *Find the Answers*
Write the letter of the correct answer.
1. Another title for Chapter 2 could be
   a. The Voyage of the *Beagle*.
   b. Moonshots for Biologists.
   c. Plants and Animals Live All Over the World.
   d. Life in the Desert . . . Life on the Moon.
2. What is the main idea of Section 2-4?
   a. Lapland's animals are unusual.
   b. Linnaeus's travels resulted in scientific knowledge.
   c. It is not necessary for a naturalist to fly or take a boat.
   d. Swedish naturalists were early explorers.
3. In Section 2-3, we read that the naturalist, Darwin,
   a. developed a system for naming tortoises.
   b. studied nature for five years.
   c. showed that birds and insects can live near coral.
   d. bought samples of nature from the natives.

4. In which environment is the bathyscaphe used?
   a. ocean
   b. desert
   c. forest
   d. Lapland
5. Which scientist developed a system for naming plants and animals?
   a. Darwin
   b. Linnaeus
   c. Beebe
   d. Aristotle

B. *Choose One*
Write the answer that correctly completes the sentence.
1. Field glasses are also called (binoculars, vasculum).
2. A scientist who was an early underwater explorer was (Darwin, Beebe).
3. Fresh plants on a field trip would probably be stored in a (vasculum, collecting jar).
4. On a field trip into the woods to observe birds a scientist might take (a microscope, binoculars).

## Word tools

Match the organisms with their correct environment. (One environment will not be used.)

**Organism**

1. lizard
2. oyster
3. tortoise
4. chipmunk
5. whale

**Environment**

a. ocean
b. Galapagos Islands
c. Lapland
d. woodland
e. seashore
f. desert

## Knowing what and why

A. *Explanation, Please . . .*
   Answer in one or two sentences.
   1. How many senses do we have? What are they?
   2. How did Darwin record his observations? Why was it important for him to keep good records?
   3. What are three organisms you are likely to see at the seashore?

B. *Do You Agree or Disagree?*
   Write a sentence stating your reasons.
   1. Darwin and Linnaeus often compared their work.
   2. It is not necessary to travel far to learn about nature.
   3. Scientists are really like explorers.

C. *Puzzling It Out*
   In a sentence or two, suggest how each piece of equipment might be used to study the animals named.

   1. binoculars for birds
   2. a tape recorder for crickets
   3. a still camera for an eagle
   4. a motion picture camera for bees

## Looking further

1. Carolus Linnaeus invented a system for classifying species of plants and animals. In his system, animals and plants were grouped by their similarities. They were given Latin (or Greek) names which usually appear in *italic* print. For example, *Felis domestica* is the name for a house cat. *Felis leo* is the name for a lion.

   Why do you think these animals were given the same "first name"? What are their likenesses, their differences? In a reference book, find out the scientific names for these organisms: dog, housefly, black bear, and corn plant.

2. In your school library, thumb through a copy of *National Geographic* magazine. Make a list of each place that is written about in the articles. Next to the location, describe the kind of environment it is. Make a list of the plants and animals living there.

## chapter 3

# *Growing things at home*

### 3-1. Living things at home

Golden hamsters breed at four months. They carry their young for 15 days and live about two years.

People have many different kinds of pets. Dogs, cats, hamsters, and parakeets are a few. Many homes have a few plants on the window sill and perhaps a fish tank. Living things are interesting. They make a home pretty and colorful. You may be interested to know that you can grow many new things at home. This will make it possible for you to observe and experiment for yourself. All this and a new hobby, too!

### 3-2. Life in an aquarium

Aquarium: *aqua*-water
Terrarium: *terre*-earth

A fish tank is also called an AQUARIUM (uh-KWARE-ee-um). An aquarium contains fish and green water plants. What are three life activities you can see in an aquarium?

The green plants take in the gas CARBON DIOXIDE and they give off OXYGEN (OK-sih-jun). Fish use oxygen and give off carbon dioxide. Fish remove oxygen from the air that is in the water. When an aquarium has the right number of fish and plants, the two live well together. The water has to be changed only once in a great while. We say then that the aquarium is *balanced*.

18

### 3-3. Life in a terrarium

A TERRARIUM (teh-RARE-ee-um) is a glass tank or bowl filled with soil, not water. In a good terrarium the soil is dark and rich. Moss plants are grown on top of the soil. Ferns grow above the soil. A terrarium is covered with glass because this keeps the air inside very moist. A few pieces of bark and a rock or two make a very attractive scene. A frog or lizard is sometimes included to complete the "family."

**Fig. 19-1**
The aquarium (left) and terrarium (right) are small "worlds" of living things. How can life go on inside these containers even when they are closed?

### 3-4. Growing plants from seeds

The seeds that some plants produce are alive and can grow into plants if they have water and proper temperature. When seeds begin growing roots and stems, we say they GERMINATE (JUR-muh-nayt). Most seeds, if soaked in water overnight, will germinate faster. Corn seeds, black beans, and pea seeds germinate fast and show roots and stems clearly.

## Do and Discover

Investigation 1: How do seeds germinate?

**Procedures**

1. Line a jar with wet blotter paper. Place seeds between the paper and the sides of the jar. Cover the jar with a saucer or glass plate. Place the jar on a dark shelf in a warm place.
2. Set up a second jar in the same way. Keep this one in the refrigerator.
3. Set up a third jar like #1, but do *not* wet the blotter paper.

**Observations and Analysis**

1. How long does it take for roots to appear in each jar? Explain.
2. What grows from the *top* of the seeds?
3. In which direction do roots grow?
4. What happened to the skin of the seed (outer seed coat)?
5. What happens when the set-up dries out?
6. Set-up #3 is called a *control*. What is its function?

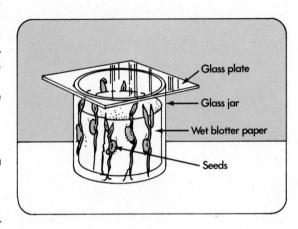

**Fig. 20-1**

---

3-5. Plants from cut stems

Many plants when cut through the stem and placed in water, soil, or sand will grow roots. Plants which are cut at the stems and then used to grow new plants are called *cuttings*. Common house plants such as the GERANIUM (jih-RAY-

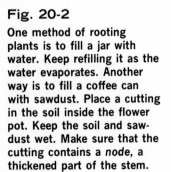

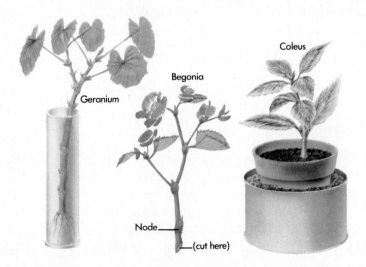

**Fig. 20-2**

One method of rooting plants is to fill a jar with water. Keep refilling it as the water evaporates. Another way is to fill a coffee can with sawdust. Place a cutting in the soil inside the flower pot. Keep the soil and sawdust wet. Make sure that the cutting contains a *node*, a thickened part of the stem.

nee-um), BEGONIA (bih-GOH-nee-uh), and COLEUS (KOH-lee-us) can be cut and regrown in this way. Each cutting will become a new plant.

### 3-6. We grow plants from parts of plants

Do you know which part of a plant you eat for food? Here are four common plants:

| Plant | Part we eat |
|---|---|
| onion | stem with leaves wrapped around it |
| sweet potato | fat, sweet root |
| white potato | underground stem |
| carrot | root |

The pictures show how parts of a plant may be used to grow a whole plant.

Sweet potato

Potato slice with eye

Carrot with bottom cut off

Onion supported by toothpicks

**Fig. 21-1**
What three conditions will be needed to make each plant grow? Try to invent an investigation to check each one.

### 3-7. Invisible living things

The air, soil, and water are filled with living things which we cannot always see with the naked eye. These are plants that must be studied with a microscope. Scientists have discovered that the air is filled with tiny SPORES (SPORZ) which, like seeds, can germinate to form tiny plants called MOLDS. Perhaps you have seen bread mold or molds on cheese or oranges. Molds spoil valuable food. For this reason, food must be kept covered or refrigerated.

## Do and Discover

Investigation 2: How can we trap and grow mold spores?

**Procedures**

1. Obtain a shallow glass baking pan. LIne its bottom with blotting paper which you have soaked in water. Lay out the foods as shown in the diagram. Leave the pan uncovered overnight.
2. The next day, cover the pan with a piece of transparent plastic. Then put it away in a dark, warm place for a few days.
3. Examine the growth with a magnifying glass.

**Observations and Analysis**

1. Describe the growths you see. What are their textures, colors, and how are they distributed?
2. Smell the growths. Describe.
3. Where did the growths come from?
4. How could you test the effects of different temperatures on the molds?
5. Can you suggest a control experiment?
6. How is mold growth usually prevented?

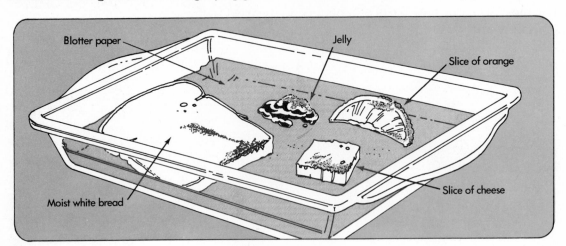

Blotter paper  Jelly  Slice of orange  Slice of cheese  Moist white bread

Fig. 22-1

## Learned So Far . . .

● Living things may be grown easily at home.

## SELF-STUDY GUIDE FOR CHAPTER 3

All answers should be written in your notebook. Please do not write in this book.

### Understanding the reading

A. *Find the Answers*
Write the letter of the correct answer.
1. What is the main idea of Chapter 3?
    a. Molds spoil bread.
    b. A terrarium is not filled with water.
    c. We can study living things at home.
    d. Many plants are grown without seeds.
2. You may have to change the water in an aquarium very often, if
    a. mold spores fall in.
    b. there are too many fish.
    c. you don't feed the fish.
    d. there are no plants in the tank.
3. The following are *not* wanted in a terrarium, except
    a. ants.
    b. molds.
    c. fish.
    d. lizards.
4. Which of the following are needed for seeds to germinate?
    a. water and warmth
    b. water and darkness
    c. water and light
    d. darkness and warmth

B. *True or False.*
If the statement is true, write *true*. If the statement is false, change the word in *italics* to make the statement true.

1. A sweet potato is an underground *stem*.
2. Mold spores land on bread from the *air*.
3. Soaking of seeds in water *speeds up* their germination.
4. The node is the swollen portion of a *root*.
5. Aquarium plants give off *oxygen*.

C. *Locate the Idea*
Find the section in which each of these questions is answered. Write the number of the section and one or two sentences that answer the question.

1. How can we keep an aquarium "balanced"?
2. What part of the onion plant do we eat?
3. How can we study the cause of moldy bread?
4. How can we grow many plants from one plant?

### Word tools

Complete each statement by choosing a word from the list. (Two words will not be used.)

1. New molds can grow from _____.
2. New geraniums can grow from _____.
3. A carrot is the _____ of the plant.
4. Mosses and ferns are found in a(n) _____.
5. Fish and green plants are found in a(n) _____.

root
germination
aquarium
spores
cuttings
terrarium
begonia

## Knowing what and why

A. *Do You Agree or Disagree?*
   Write a sentence stating your reasons.
   1. A control is important to an investigation.
   2. All plants are grown from cuttings.
   3. Underground stems may be eaten as food.
B. *Analyzing the Investigation*
   Study Investigation 1. Answer the following questions in one or two sentences.
   1. Why was the second jar put into the refrigerator?
   2. What effect does cold have on germinating seeds?
   3. Would the third jar still be a control if water was added? Why or why not?
   4. How might you do an experiment testing the effect of *light* on germinating seeds?

## Looking further

Set up the two experiments as shown. Make daily observations. Enter them in your notebook. How can we raise earthworms? How can we develop ant colonies?

**Fig. 24-1**

Fill half of a large jar with a mixture of soil, decayed leaves, grass, lettuce, and coffee grounds. After a heavy rain, you can usually find some worms on the surface of a garden or near a bush. Drop two or three worms into the mixture. Keep it moist but not too wet. Keep the jar covered with a screen or a piece of cheese cloth.

Your "mix" here is moist, sandy soil. Drop a small ant hill into the jar. Wrap brown paper around the jar. For food, add tiny bits of lettuce, carrot, and scraps of meat. Remove food which is not used. When you want to observe the ants, remove the brown wrapper.

How are living things affected by their environment?
How do living things affect each other?

# Life in the environment

## 4-1. The home of living things

Take a look around you. You see living things everywhere.
Living things share the earth—the land, the water, and the
air above the land and water. But living things cannot live
very far below the surface of the earth. Nor do they live high
above in the layer of air that surrounds the earth. This
shallow layer where animals and plants can live is called the
BIOSPHERE (BY-uh-sfeer). It is the home of life on Earth.

When we study life in the biosphere we are studying
ECOLOGY (ih-KOL-uh-jee). ECOLOGISTS (ih-KOL-uh-
jists) learn about the *relationships* of one kind of living thing
to all other living things. They also study how living things
are affected by the *nonliving* parts of the biosphere.

Fig. 25-1
The angelfish and the side-
winder snake live in different
parts of the biosphere. How
would you describe each of
their homes?

25

### 4-2. On land and in the water

Plants and animals live in different "sections" of the biosphere. Each of these sections is called a BIOME (BY-ohm). Ecologists have divided the earth into six *land* biomes and two *water* biomes.

As you can guess, the two water biomes are the *freshwater* (rivers and lakes) and the *marine* (salt water oceans and bays). The land biomes differ according to the temperatures and the water found in each. The chart shows you the major "homes" of living things.

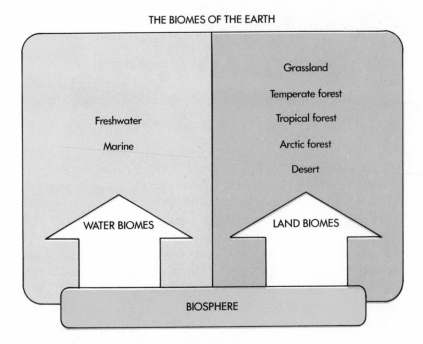

THE BIOMES OF THE EARTH

**Fig. 26-1**

### 4-3. Living and nonliving factors

In the biosphere all living things affect each other. For example, a rabbit is affected by the amounts and kinds of grass and other plants in its environment. It is also affected by the presence of animals like foxes or wolves.

But life is also controlled by *nonliving* factors. For example, the same rabbit would be affected if the temperature dropped suddenly, or if the stream nearby dried up. The chart shows the nonliving factors in the environment which affect living things.

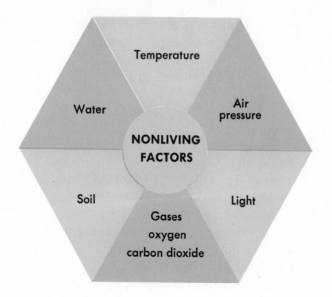

**Fig. 27-1**

Give one example of how each factor may affect living things.

## 4-4. Life in an "envelope of air"

The envelope of air which surrounds the earth is the AT-MOSPHERE (AT-muh-sfeer). The atmosphere extends about 800 km above the earth. Our weather is found in the closest layer of the atmosphere. This layer is made up of a mixture of gases. About 20% of the air at the earth's surface is oxygen.

All animals need oxygen. Animals living in deep caves or even ants crawling along the sidewalk must have oxygen. Land animals breathe oxygen from the air. AQUATIC (uh-KWAT-ik) animals absorb it from the water.

## Learned So Far . . .

- There is life on land, in the air, and in the water.
- Life is affected by the living and nonliving parts of the environment.
- Ecology is the study of the relationships among living things.

## 4-5. How does light control life?

Light energy travels from the sun to the earth—a distance of 150 000 000 km. Sunlight reaches the earth in 8.3 minutes. Only part of the sun's energy is useful to life.

The most important use of light is by green plants. They use it to make food in their leaves. Land plants adapt to the amount of light which is available to them. Some plants grow best in bright sun. Others can grow in the dim light of a forest.

What about plants in the water, especially deep oceans? Sunlight usually passes through ocean water to a depth of 80 m. There seems to be no light below 200 m. Would you find plant life below this depth?

Animals are affected by light, too. Don't animals that eat green plants depend on the sun *indirectly* for food? But light also affects animals *directly,* mostly in their behavior and appearance. For example, fish that live near the ocean surface may have lighter color than those living far below the surface. How some animals multiply, or BREED, depends on light. As daylight increases in the spring, many animals begin their breeding season.

Chicken farmers keep lights on in the hen houses during the hours of darkness. The hens respond to the light by laying more eggs.

### 4-6. How does temperature affect life?

Temperature affects the chemical action in living things. Low temperatures can freeze the water in living material. Every autumn, when temperatures drop, many plants die. Rising temperatures in the spring "call the plants to life" again. Refrigeration kills germs. High temperatures do also. Temperature also affects behavior. For example, bears and chipmunks go to sleep for the winter. This behavior is called HIBERNATION (hy-bur-NAY-shun). Animals hibernate in winter to withstand the cold. During hibernation, life activities slow down. The heartbeat slows. Breathing almost stops. Similarly, some animals go to sleep for the *summer* to withstand the high heat.

Do humans respond to temperature changes? Of course! Many of us slow down on very hot days. We shiver and develop "goose pimples" when we are very cold. Excessive cold can also slow down body functions.

**Fig. 28-1**

In the winter this bear will go into hibernation. Before that it will eat all it can to prepare for the cold weather. How does hibernation help animals survive?

### 4-7. Temperatures . . . here and there

Temperatures are different in different parts of the land and in different parts of the oceans. The snow never melts on high mountains. Water rarely freezes in tropical and desert areas.

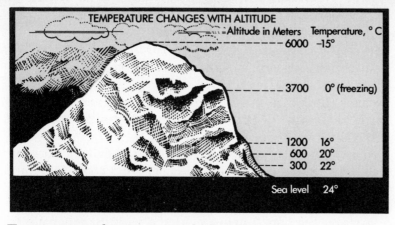

Fig. 29-1

Temperatures drop as you go higher above sea level. The drop in temperature is about 2°C for each 300 m above sea level.

## 4-8. In search of food

The search for food is a never-ending job of living organisms.

Green plants make their own food. They are PRODUC-ERS. Most animals use plants and other animals for food. They are CONSUMERS. Some, like bacteria, feed on dead material, causing it to decay. These are the DECOMPOS-ERS (dee-kum-POH-zurz). When we show how plants and animals depend on each other for food we describe a FOOD CHAIN. See Fig. 29-2.

## 4-9. The struggle for existence

How do living things get along with each other? All living things reproduce their own kind. In fact all living things *overproduce* in reproduction. Dandelions produce millions of seeds. Fish produce millions of eggs. In fact, if every seed and every egg produced a live offspring, the world would quickly

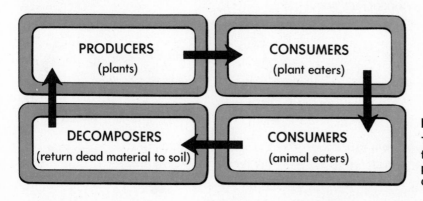

Fig. 29-2

The general pattern of a food chain. What might happen if we ever broke this chain?

be overrun. But, even with overproduction, the total population of the world does not change that greatly. Why? Because there is a "fight" to survive. There is COMPETITION (kom-pih-TISH-un). In Darwin's words, there is "a struggle for existence."

What is this fight about? What is the struggle for? It is for the materials and conditions of life. There is competition for food, water, oxygen, space, and a mate. In addition, all species have natural enemies and compete to escape from them.

Can you see how humans compete with all other life to survive? Do humans always win?

## Learned So Far . . .

- Light and temperature control life activities.
- Living things use each other in the search for food.
- In every biome, there is a struggle for existence among the "residents."

## Do and Discover

Investigation 3: How do animals respond to light?

### Procedures

1. Obtain a milk bottle and cover it with black construction paper. Hold the paper in place with rubber bands.
2. The live specimens used will depend on where you live. Many pet shops sell an organism known as *DAPHNIA* (DAF-nee-uh) for fish food. If you live near a pond you can also catch your own Daphnia (or use brine shrimp).
3. Fill the bottle with fresh water and add about 30 Daphnia. Make sure they are swimming in all directions.
4. Shine a flashlight on the surface for 10 minutes.
5. Remove the black paper and observe.
6. Try the experiment without the light.

### Observations and Analysis

1. Are the animals attracted to the light?
2. Daphnia live in freshwater ponds. Give some

reasons why you feel they react to light in this manner.
3. Is there a control in this experiment? Explain.

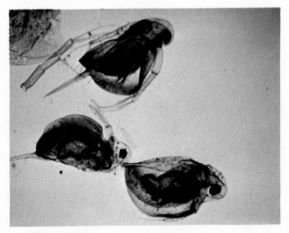

**Fig. 30-1**

Daphnia can be observed more closely with the help of magnification.

## SELF-STUDY GUIDE FOR CHAPTER 4

All answers should be written in your notebook. Please do not write in this book.

### Understanding the reading

A.  *Find the Answers*
Write the letter of the correct answer.
1. What is the main idea of Chapter 4?
   a. The biosphere is the home of life.
   b. All life is related to each other.
   c. Nonliving factors can kill all life.
   d. Green plants are superior to all other life.
2. The part of our planet which makes up the home of living things is the
   a. biome.
   b. forest.
   c. atmosphere.
   d. biosphere.
3. The life of a deer is affected *only* by
   a. other deer in the area.
   b. all animals in the area.
   c. all plants and animals in the area.
   d. the living and nonliving factors in the area.
4. Bacteria generally get their food by
   a. killing living things.
   b. making it from raw materials.
   c. a process not yet known.
   d. breaking down dead organisms.
5. A food chain shows the relationship between
   a. living and nonliving factors.
   b. water and land biomes.
   c. producers and consumers.
   d. competition and hibernation.

B.  *Locate the Idea*
Find the section in which each of these questions is answered. Write the number of the section and one or two sentences that answer the question.
1. Why do plants begin to grow again in the spring?
2. Why are bacteria often found in dead animals?
3. What kind of biome is formed by rivers and lakes?
4. What do plants and animals compete for in their efforts to survive?

### Word tools

Find the correct definition from *Column B* which describes the term in *Column A*. (One definition will not be used.)

**Column A**
1. biosphere
2. biome
3. ecology
4. nonliving factors
5. consumer organism

**Column B**
a. study of relationships of life with other life
b. a special kind of environment
c. space biology
d. uses plants and animals for food
e. water, soil, air, light, and temperature
f. the "total" home of life

### Knowing what and why

A.  *Do You Agree or Disagree?*
Write a sentence stating your reasons.

1. All life depends on the sun directly or indirectly.

2. Cutting down forests may affect soil.
3. Zoo keepers often have trouble maintaining imported animals.
4. Bacteria are always harmful.
5. The overproduction of young hurts the population of an organism.
6. In the struggle for existence, humans will always win.

B. *Understanding the Pictures*
   1. Look back to Figure 26-1. Which of these biomes do you live in? Which biomes would be found in very cold parts of the earth? Which would be found near the equator?

2. Look back to Figure 29-1. What temperature might you find at an altitude of 1200 meters? 3700 meters? Do you think that the biome changes as you go up the side of a mountain? Why?

C. *On the Ladder of Understanding*
   Answer these questions in a sentence or two. You may wish to review earlier chapters.
   1. Why are green plants needed in an aquarium?
   2. Is seeing the only way of observing? Explain.
   3. Why are biologists like explorers?

*Looking further*———————————————————————

1. Start your own nature collection. Collect leaves from some of the plants found in your neighborhood. Paste them on cardboard and write a description of how each looks according to color, shape, size, and texture. Try to find out their names.
2. Create your own biome in a shoe box. Pick one of the biomes of the world and find out what plants and animals live there. Use your imagination to make a model of that biome.
3. Do you own a camera? Start a collection of nature photos. A good start is getting photos of animals and plants mentioned so far in Chapters 1 through 4. Bring your collection to class. If you don't have a camera, cut out pictures from magazines.

# UNIT II

# *The scientist at work*

## Unit II/outline

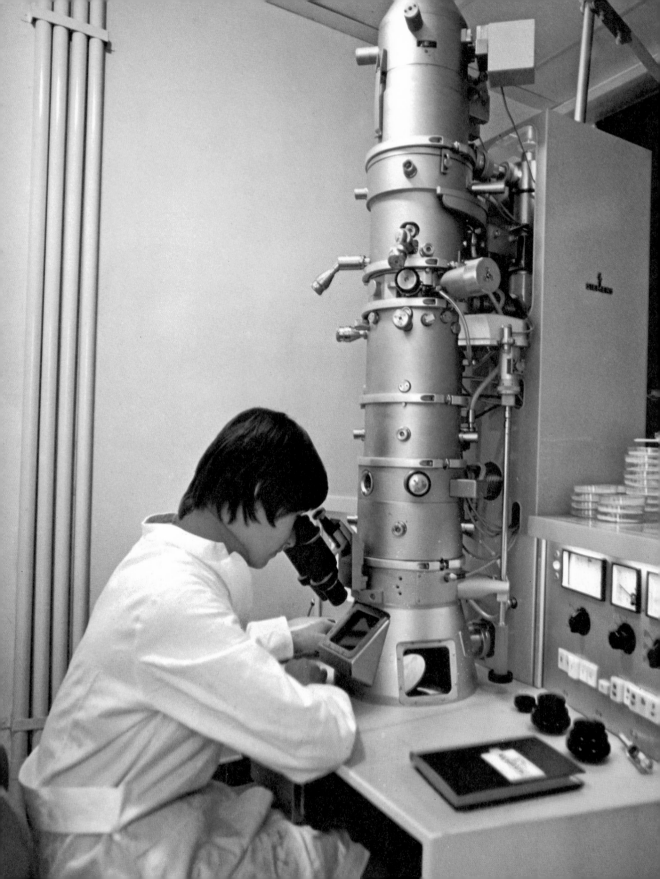

# *The scientist at work*

## What's it all about?

Have you ever wondered why a rosebud opens? Or why the birds come back in the spring? The riddles of nature can be unlocked, if we *search*. The ways of life can be made clearer if we *investigate*. Human wisdom, with patience, can solve the problems around us.

This is what science is all about. The scientist works in many places and in many ways. Scientists have invented all kinds of tools and instruments to help the human senses.

The work must be careful and precise. Sometimes it can be very, very slow. Other times, an idea is born suddenly. Sometimes a scientist even has a lucky break and "stumbles" upon an answer.

In this unit, you will learn
- how scientists get answers to questions.
- what goes on in a science laboratory.
- where scientists work.
- about some tools and instruments used by scientists.
- about the use of numbers and measurements needed in science.

*And just as important,* you will learn
- how *you* can do science investigations.
- how *you* can use science tools and take measurements.
- that the work of scientists is *never* done, because they do not know all the answers.

## chapter 5

# The scientist in search of answers

QUESTIONS

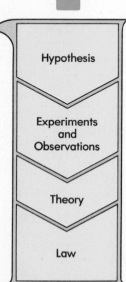

Hypothesis

Experiments and Observations

Theory

Law

Fig. 36-1

### 5-1. Let's study science

Whenever we study natural things, both around us and directly connected with us, we are studying *science*. Scientists study the environment in a very special way. They start out with questions and look for answers. Scientists *investigate* by collecting facts. As in other fields, scientists try to come to conclusions.

But science is also different from other subjects. Science depends much more heavily on *careful observation*. Scientific observation means recognizing and noting facts. Scientists know that the five human senses are not perfect. So they often depend on instruments to check their observations. In this way, the answers that scientists get from their observations come closer to being accurate. Scientists carefully plan how to get facts with EXPERIMENTS.

### 5-2. How do scientists discover answers?

How does a scientist get answers to questions? Like detective work, the search starts with a "hunch." In science, we call this a HYPOTHESIS (hy-POTH-ih-sis). It is not a wild guess. The hypothesis may be based on previous experience. Perhaps it is based on reading or talking with other scientists.

Now the experiments begin. Observations are made. Facts are collected. Facts are tested. Sometimes scientists try out certain answers or solutions and find that they are wrong. So they try again. By trying out many wrong answers and solutions, scientists sometimes finally find the right one. We call this method of experimenting TRIAL AND ERROR.

From this work may come a THEORY (THEE-uh-ree). The theory is "stronger" than the hypothesis. It has more facts to back it up. Sometimes a theory becomes so strong that there are few exceptions. We now have a scientific LAW.

When is the scientist's work really done? Old laws may be changed or thrown out. New theories may arise. More experiments may show new ideas. If you say "The scientist's work is never done," you are right!

## 5-3. The many branches of science

Long ago, early scientists studied many different fields. As more and more answers were found, they began to pay closer attention to a smaller number of questions—and even to only one bit of knowledge. They became SPECIALISTS (SPESH-uh-lists). They became experts in one small branch of science. Today, there are hundreds of branches of science. The charts show only a few.

As you may have guessed, many sciences are related. Can biology be studied without reference to the other sciences? Can a biologist explain how the eyes work without knowing about lenses and light? The answer is *no*. A good biologist must also have an understanding of the *physical* sciences.

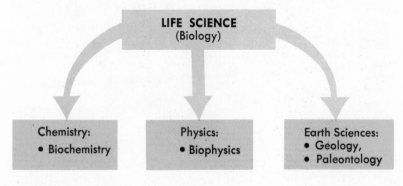

Fig. 37-1

## Fig. 38-1

Look up the following words in the dictionary: optics, metallurgy, thermodynamics, seismograph, acoustics, herbivore. Then, in your notebook, place each word under the correct branch of science, copied from the chart.

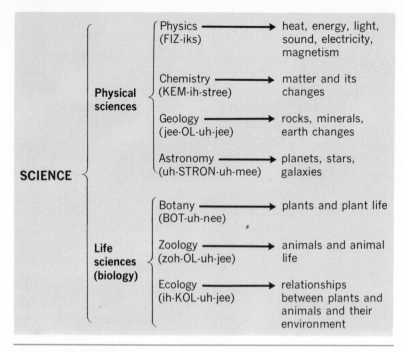

SCIENCE

**Physical sciences**

Physics (FIZ-iks) → heat, energy, light, sound, electricity, magnetism

Chemistry (KEM-ih-stree) → matter and its changes

Geology (jee-OL-uh-jee) → rocks, minerals, earth changes

Astronomy (uh-STRON-uh-mee) → planets, stars, galaxies

**Life sciences (biology)**

Botany (BOT-uh-nee) → plants and plant life

Zoology (zoh-OL-uh-jee) → animals and animal life

Ecology (ih-KOL-uh-jee) → relationships between plants and animals and their environment

## Learned So Far . . .

- Scientists learn by careful observations and experiments to obtain accurate answers.
- Scientists start with questions and temporary answers (hypotheses). Then they move to theories and laws.
- Science study is now specialized into many related branches.

## Fig. 38-2

This laboratory is a scientist's workshop. Which step in the scientific process is this scientist most likely performing?

## 5-4. In the laboratory

Look at the word *laboratory.* The first part, *labor,* gives the clue. Yes, it is a *work* shop—a busy place that is well equipped with instruments, chemicals, plants, animals, books, and other supplies.

Who works in a laboratory? There are scientists, secretaries, laboratory assistants, and technicians. In some biology labs, there are animal handlers and *horticulturists* (plant-breeders).

A biology laboratory may be a private laboratory or part of a college. It may be a hospital laboratory. Many businesses, such as dairies, breweries, drug companies, and cheese factories, have their own laboratories. Government laboratories like those of the Department of Agriculture and the Public Health Service are well known.

There are many jobs in laboratories for which only a high-school education is needed.

As we saw, ideas in biology depend on ideas in physics and chemistry. Therefore, it should not surprise us to learn that many experiments in a life-science laboratory are also experiments in physics and chemistry.

Suppose a biologist wants to know what is happening to the fish in a river near a manufacturing plant. Samples of the water from the river would have to be tested for the presence of substances coming from the plant. Chemistry and physics would play an important part in the biologist's experiments.

## 5-5. Talking it over . . . reading all about it

Biologists cannot work alone. They depend on hearing what other biologists are doing and learning. Each year biologists get together at meetings or *conventions* held all over the world. At these conventions, scientists give talks and show slides of their work. Often they *present a paper* about their research. Scientists find this kind of sharing very helpful.

Scientists publish their experiments in science *journals* (magazines) and in books. They read the journals in their field so that they know what is new.

**Fig. 39-1**
On this farm, the farmer and the veterinarian apply their scientific knowledge.

## 5-6. Biology on the job

People involved in life science do more than *find* answers. They also *use* answers. This is *applied biology.* Applied

biology is found in hospitals. There technicians study blood, viruses, and X-rays. Biology is also active on farms where soil improvement, plant and animal breeding, and insect control are important.

There are biologists in food factories and in environmental protection agencies. They are in fish hatcheries and forests. Yes, biology is a practical and useful science.

**Fig. 40-1**

A greenhouse may be a plant laboratory. What problems do you think are solved here?

## Learned So Far . . .

- Scientists work in laboratories: private, college, industrial, or governmental.
- Scientists also work in libraries and at conventions.
- Biology is an applied, practical science, useful to the work of hospitals, farms, and industry.

## Do and Discover

Investigation 4: What are some simple chemical tests which answer scientific questions?

**Procedures**

1. Place a drop of bicarbonate of soda mixture on a piece of *red* litmus paper. Observe.
2. Repeat with a drop of vinegar on *blue* litmus paper. Observe.
3. Place a piece of red litmus paper under your tongue for a couple of minutes. Observe.
4. Place a piece of PTC paper in your mouth. What do you taste?
5. Pour 15 mL of the dye, *methyl orange*, into each of two test tubes. To the first test tube,

add a few drops of bicarbonate of soda. Observe. To the second test tube, add a few drops of vinegar. Observe.

**Observations and Analysis**

1. Record your observations in table form.
2. Which of the materials you used is called a *base*? Which is an *acid*?
3. Did everyone get the same taste with PTC paper? Explain.

## SELF-STUDY GUIDE FOR CHAPTER 5

All answers should be written in your notebook. Please do not write in this book.

## Understanding the reading

A. *Find the Answers*

Write the letter of the correct answer.
1. What is the main idea of Chapter 5?
   a. Scientists work very hard in their labs.

b. A knowledge of biology helps us in useful ways.
c. Scientists use careful observations and tests to develop answers to questions.

d. Governments are in the "science business."

2. "Trial and error" in scientific work
   a. may mean long delays before answers.
   b. signals the scientist to give up.
   c. leads quickly to new answers.
   d. shows that our instruments and tests are very poor.

3. A scientific "law"
   a. can never be wrong.
   b. is much like a hypothesis.
   c. may be changed.
   d. guides scientists in the kind of work they are allowed to do.

4. Geology and astronomy are
   a. both physical sciences.
   b. both branches of biology.
   c. applied sciences in industry.
   d. branches of ecology.

B.  Locate the Idea
Find the sentence which answers each question. Write the sentence in your notebook.
1. Section 5-2: When is a scientist's work done?
2. Section 5-3: What do we call scientists who become experts in one small area of science?
3. Section 5-4: Name *five* kinds of employees found in some science labs.
4. Section 5-5: What do we call a meeting where scientists gather?

## Word tools

In the following words, what does the underlined part mean? Write your answers in your notebook. (You may use a dictionary.)

1. specia<u>list</u>    2. <u>geo</u>logy    3. <u>zoo</u>logy    4. <u>labora</u>tory    5. <u>astro</u>nomy

## Knowing what and why

A.  Explanation, Please. . .
Answer in one or two sentences.
1. A hypothesis is "weaker" than a theory.
2. Applied biology is not the only valuable kind of biology.
3. A scientist may do an experiment many times before announcing a new theory.
4. A library is important to a scientist.

B.  What's the Difference?
In a sentence or two, explain the difference between the two words in each pair.
1. zoology–botany
2. theory–hypothesis
3. observation–conclusion

C.  Analyzing the Investigation
Study Investigation 4. Answer the questions below.

1. In step 4, how do you know that it is not some leftover food in your mouth which is producing the result?

2. Is there a difference in PTC tasting between males and females? Between people of different races? How can you find out?

3. How does this experiment show that chemistry is an important part of studying biology?

## Looking further

1. Watch your newspapers for announcements of a special TV program called *Nova*. This deals with scientific subjects. You will enjoy watching it. Discuss with your class.

2. Your teacher may be able to arrange a class trip to a local hospital lab.

**TARGET:** What instruments are used in a laboratory?

# *Tools in the laboratory*

### 6-1. Using instruments in the laboratory

In order to carry out experiments, scientists need many kinds of instruments. Some instruments help scientists get accurate answers by measuring or weighing the results of their experiments. Some instruments are used to control the growth of living things, so that living things can be better understood. Where do these instruments come from? There are hundreds of factories that employ thousands of workers who make the instruments used by scientists. Some day, you may be able to get a job in this field.

**Fig. 42-1**

Can you name some scientific tools that a life scientist would "borrow" from a physics or chemistry laboratory?

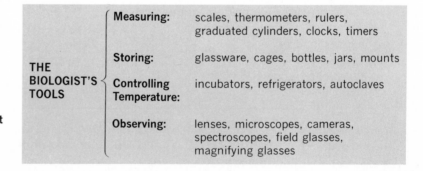

| THE BIOLOGIST'S TOOLS | Measuring: | scales, thermometers, rulers, graduated cylinders, clocks, timers |
| | Storing: | glassware, cages, bottles, jars, mounts |
| | Controlling Temperature: | incubators, refrigerators, autoclaves |
| | Observing: | lenses, microscopes, cameras, spectroscopes, field glasses, magnifying glasses |

## 6-2. Chemical tests explain life's processes

Did you know that if you breathe into a clear solution of limewater that the solution will turn cloudy? This shows that our exhaled air contains *carbon dioxide* gas. It has been known for a long time that living things can react to chemicals and will show certain changes. This is of great help when we study plants and animals. For example, there is a chemical test called URINALYSIS (yoor-ih-NAL-uh-sis). URINE (YOOR-in) is the liquid waste of animals (including humans). If the analysis shows traces of sugar in someone's urine, this indicates that the person has a disease called DIABETES (dy-uh-BEE-teez).

## 6-3. A look inside living things

Have you ever taken a toy apart? Or an old clock? You were curious and wanted to know how it worked. Scientists also want to look inside plants and animals to see "how they work." They do careful cutting called DISSECTION (dy-SEK-shun).

When scientists dissect plants, they can study the insides of roots and stems. In animals, they can see how muscles are attached to bones or how many sections a brain has.

---

## Learned So Far . . .

* Instruments and special tools are used by the scientist in the lab.
* Chemical tests are used in the study of biology.
* Dissection shows us the "insides" of plants and animals.

---

## 6-4. How big? How long? How wide?

How high is an oak tree? How long is an earthworm? These are simple questions you can answer easily by measuring with a ruler or with a measuring tape.

We say the human appendix is about 7.5 centimeters (ab-

**Fig. 43-1**
Dissecting is a careful art that takes skill and patience. These are its tools.

---

Scientists are careful not to cause pain to animals. They use painkillers or put the animal "to sleep" in a painless way.

---

**Fig. 43-2**
The ruler shows centimeters and inches. Metric rulers are found in various lengths. The meter stick is for a carpenter. The tape measure is for a tailor or road surveyor. (See page 173 for a table that compares metric measurement to English measurement.)

breviated cm) long. The giant redwood trees in our national parks tower to a height of 109 m. In each case, we are measuring distance in a straight line. Such measurements of length, width, and height are called LINEAR (LIN-ee-ur) measurements. The amount of surface or area that something has is figured using its linear measurements. A leaf may have 8 square centimeters of surface (8 cm$^2$). A farmer grows beans on one HECTARE (HEK-tair) of land (10,000 m$^2$).

### 6-5. How much does it "weigh"?

What you are really asking is, "How much *mass* (or material) has it?" In ordinary language we may use the words *weigh* or *weight*.

Weighing living things or their parts is another form of investigating. For example, which has more mass—a cat's brain or a monkey's brain? Does a diseased kidney have more or less mass than a healthy kidney?

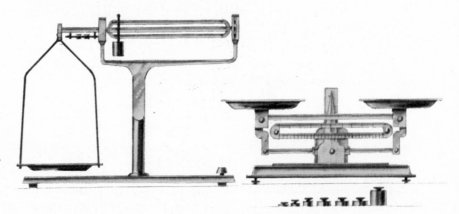

**Fig. 44-2**

A laboratory balance (left) and a beam balance (right).

A *scale* will tell you. A scale might be used by a biologist to find the mass of a seed or the mass of a diseased organ. Different kinds of scales (or *balances*) are used for different jobs. The delicate laboratory balance is used to find the mass of small objects. A beam balance is used to find the masses of larger objects.

### 6-6. How much space?

How much space does a bone cell take up? How much space

does the blood in our bodies occupy? How much air can a lung hold? The amount of space taken up by a solid (like the bone cell), by a liquid (like the blood), or by a gas (like the air in the lungs) is called VOLUME (VOL-yoom).

How do we find the volume of an object? If the object is solid and has a regular shape, like a brick, it has length, width, and height. The volume of solids is measured in cubic centimeters ($cm^3$) or in cubic meters ($m^3$). The figures show how easy it is to find the volume of a solid.

| THE VOLUME OF A BOX |
| --- |
| **Volume** = length × width × height |
| **Volume** = 8 cm × 4 cm × 3 cm |
| **Volume** = 96 $cm^3$ |

### 6-7. How much does it hold?

The volume of a solid can be figured by measurements. But liquids and gases are more difficult to measure. They have no shape of their own and spread out to fill their containers. Therefore, we measure the volume of liquids and gases by finding out how much their containers hold.

In the kitchen we use a measuring cup with markings on it. In a laboratory we use a beaker or a *graduated* (marked) cylinder.

The volume of liquids and gases may be expressed in milliliters (mL). A beaker may be of 500 mL, 1000 mL, or 5000 mL size. A kitchen measuring dispenser might be of 5 mL, 25 mL, or even 250 mL size.

### 6-8. How hot is it? How cold is it?

Have you seen tropical fish in a tank? These fish are very sensitive to the cold. The water in the tank must be kept warm by a special heater. All living things are affected by changes in temperature. Temperature is measured in degrees with an instrument called a THERMOMETER (thur-MOM-ih-tur). See Fig. 46-1.

The degree of heat is read on a CELSIUS (SEL-see-us) scale. The higher the number, the higher the temperature.

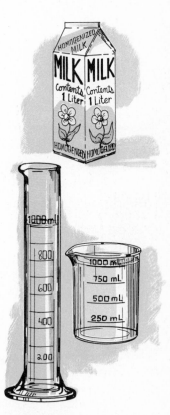

**Fig. 45-1**
Three shapes, three sizes, but the same volume of liquid. Explain.

### Learned So Far . . .

- Scientists use instruments for measuring mass, distance, temperature, and volume.

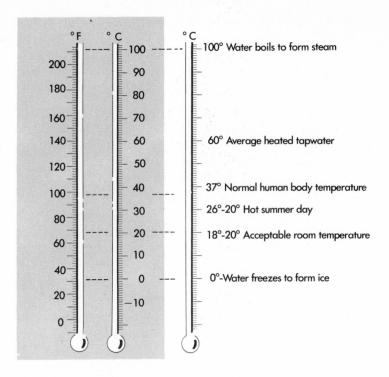

**Fig. 46-1**

Compare Celsius degrees with Fahrenheit degrees. Then study the second drawing for common temperature controls on the Celsius thermometer. Why do you think Celsius degrees are easier to memorize than Fahrenheit degrees?

°F    °C

200
180
160
140
120
100
80
60
40
20
0

100
90
80
70
60
50
40
30
20
10
0
-10

°C

100° Water boils to form steam

60° Average heated tapwater

37° Normal human body temperature

26°-20° Hot summer day

18°-20° Acceptable room temperature

0°-Water freezes to form ice

# SELF-STUDY GUIDE FOR CHAPTER 6

All answers should be written in your notebook. Please do not write in this book.

## *Understanding the reading*

A. *Find the Answers*

Write the letter of the correct answer.

1. Another title for this chapter could be
   a. Careful Tests Bring Good Results.
   b. What Scientists Use in the Biology Laboratory.
   c. Scientists Also Take Measurements.
   d. Mathematics Is Useful in Science

2. Which of these would be used for *linear* measurement?
   a. Celsius thermometer
   b. graduated cylinder
   c. metric ruler
   d. beam balance

3. Different kinds of balances are described in the section called _____ .

a. How much does it hold?
b. Chemical tests explain life processes.
c. How much does it weigh?
d. A look inside living things.

4. Why might a scientist make a *dissection*?
   a. to prove that limewater turns cloudy with carbon dioxide
   b. to see how muscles are attached to the bones
   c. to test for diabetes
   d. to find the volume of a gas

B. *Locate the Idea*

Find the section in which each of these questions is answered. Write the number of the section and one or two sentences that answer the question.

1. Why is the volume of a gas measured in a container?
2. Although we use the word *weight*, what are we really measuring?
3. Which chemical test shows the presence of sugar in urine?
4. What are we measuring when we measure area?

## Word tools

Find the correct definition in *Column B* which describes the word in *Column A*. (One definition will not be used.)

**Column A**

1. graduated cylinder
2. milliliter (mL)
3. volume
4. mass
5. hectare

**Column B**

a. 10,000 square meters
b. amount of matter in a container
c. container for measuring liquids
d. amount of matter in any material
e. a Celsius scale
f. unit for measuring liquid

## Knowing what and why

A. *Do You Agree or Disagree?*
   Write a sentence stating your reasons.
   1. Dissection is really not important. After all, x-rays show you the bones inside.
   2. It is important to measure the amount of a chemical used in a chemical test.
   3. Glassware is used to hold liquids only.
   4. A hand on the forehead is good enough to detect fever.

B. *Understanding the Diagram*
   Look back to Fig. 45-1. Answer the questions below.
   1. Do all three containers have the same amount of matter? How do you know?
   2. Suppose your friend challenges you. How could you prove your answer?

C. *Is Seeing Always Believing?*
   Examine the diagram.
   1. Which lines appears longer, AB or CD; EF or GH?

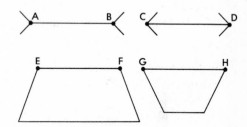

   2. Now measure each line with a metric ruler.
   3. Explain why this proves that scientists need instruments.

## Looking further

1. Look up *Anders Celsius* in an encyclopedia. Prepare a short biography to present to your class.

2. Pick up your baby brother or baby sister. Can you guess his or her mass? Now weigh the child on a scale. How close was your guess to the actual mass?

## chapter 7

# Taking measurements ...keeping records

### 7-1. Record keeping in science

Like all other people, scientists cannot always remember all of their observations. They cannot remember all the numbers they collect. What is the answer? Good records, of course.

Scientists keep records of what they observe by writing in a notebook. Quite often they also make drawings of what they see. Scientists then can compare their own observations with those of other scientists. In addition to diagrams, modern scientists also use cameras and slow-motion photography as a way of keeping records. They also use tape recorders to catch the sounds of animals.

### 7-2. Student scientists also keep records

As a science student, you most likely have a notebook for what you learn in science class. If you can draw, why not add a sketch of what you see? If you have a camera, you may want to take pictures of what you observe. Keeping good records is a helpful tool for learning.

**Fig. 48-1**

A page from the notebook of the scientist Charles Darwin. Why is a notebook important to a scientist?

### Learned So Far . . .

● Record keeping is important for scientists.
● Keeping a notebook is also important for the science student.

Fig. 49-1
Students and scientists may work in teams, one to record observations, the other to conduct the experiment.

## 7-3. Measurements and numbers in life science

The carpenter's eyes may be good—but not good enough. A level and measuring tape help a carpenter make more careful measurements. Good cooks can *estimate*. But for better results, they *measure* all ingredients.

Good workers treasure their tools. Good scientists treasure their instruments because they help them to get PRECISE (prih-SYS) measurements.

Measurements mean numbers. For example, we speak of a jogger running a distance of *50* meters in a time of *20* seconds on a day when the temperature is *17°*C.

## 7-4. Collecting data

Suppose you found a leaf on the ground. By examining it, you would see that the leaf had "teeth" on the edge. How many teeth? You could count the number of teeth on the leaf and record it in your notebook. Then you might find out if all the teeth were of the same length by measuring them. When you finished you would have a collection of facts and numbers. A collection of facts or numbers is called DATA (DAY-tuh).

## 7-5. Arranging data

Most of us can see things better when they are arranged in an

Fig. 49-2

orderly way. We often arrange numbers in *columns* or *tables*. When data are arranged in tables it is easier to *compare* two sets of numbers. Figure 50-1 shows data that were collected and then arranged into a table.

| AGE AND WEIGHT OF JAMES GREEN | | |
|---|---|---|
| Age in Years | Weight in Kilograms | Kilograms Gained Each Year |
| At Birth | 3.5 | |
| 1 | 7.0 | 3.5 |
| 2 | 11.0 | 4.0 |
| 3 | 13.5 | 2.5 |
| 4 | 15.5 | 2.0 |
| 5 | 17.6 | 2.1 |
| 6 | 21.6 | 4.0 |
| 7 | 24.5 | 2.9 |
| 8 | 26.6 | 2.1 |
| 9 | 29.1 | 2.5 |
| 10 | 33.4 | 4.3 |

Fig. 50-1

What was the weight of James Green at age 7? In which year did he have the largest weight gain? Why are tables used for this type of data?

A *graph* is a way of giving information in a kind of picture. Graphs may show the same data you find on tables and charts. However, graphs are often easier to read. Some of the many kinds of graphs are shown at the end of this chapter.

## Learned So Far . . .

● Scientists make measurements and record numbers.
● Numbers are collected to form data.
● Groups of numbers are organized into tables or graphs.

## 7-6. Standards of measurement

All throughout history, people have developed systems of measurement. In old England an *inch* was the length of three barleycorns (seeds) laid end to end. This distance was the *standard* for an inch. All systems use a standard to which you compare your own measurement.

Today scientists have more precise standards. For example, the standard length of the *meter* is actually a measurement of a certain beam of orange light.

Every measuring system has UNITS. The *meter,* the *gram,* and the *second* are examples of units. There are small units for small amounts and larger units for larger amounts.

Metal bars were once used as standards of length. But their lengths changed slightly with temperature changes. The orange light rays given off by the element *krypton* do not change.

## 7-7. The metric system

The METRIC (MEH-trik) units of measurement are used in almost all countries and in all scientific work. This system is often called SI. SI stands for the French phrase, *"Le Système International d'Unités"* (International System of Units).

The metric system is a *decimal* system. All units are related by being 10 times, 100 times, or 1000 times that of another unit. Or, to put it another way, all units are 1/10th, 1/100th, or 1/1000th of a related unit.

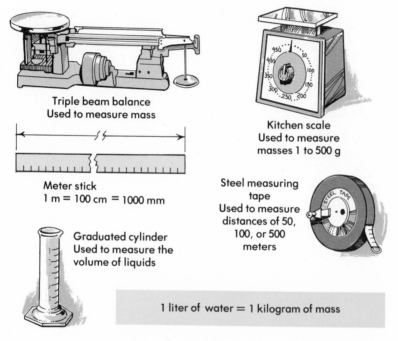

Triple beam balance
Used to measure mass

Meter stick
1 m = 100 cm = 1000 mm

Kitchen scale
Used to measure
masses 1 to 500 g

Graduated cylinder
Used to measure the
volume of liquids

Steel measuring
tape
Used to measure
distances of 50,
100, or 500
meters

1 liter of water = 1 kilogram of mass

**Fig. 51-1**

"Metric makes it 10 times easier, 100 times faster and 1000 times better." Explain this quotation.

The chart on page 52 lists the most important units of metric measurement. Read it and study it a bit. You need not memorize it. As you work with it you will become more comfortable and skilled in its use.

## Learned So Far . . .

- Measurements must be standard.
- The standard accepted throughout most of the world is the metric system.

| READY REFERENCES FOR METRIC MEASUREMENT | | | |
|---|---|---|---|
| **PURPOSE** | **MEASUREMENT** | **SYMBOL** | **EQUIVALENT** |
| FOR LENGTH OR DISTANCE | KILOMETER (KIL-uh-mee-tur)<br>METER* (MEE-tur)<br>CENTIMETER (SEN-tuh-mee-tur)<br>MILLIMETER (MIL-uh-mee-tur) | km<br>m<br>cm<br>mm | 1 km = 1000 m<br>1 m = 100 cm<br>1 cm = 10 mm |
| AREA OR SURFACE | SQUARE KILOMETER<br>HECTARE (HEK-tair)<br>SQUARE METER<br>SQUARE CENTIMETER | km²<br>ha<br>m²<br>cm² | 1 km × 1 km<br>10 000 m²<br>1 m × 1 m<br>1 cm × 1 cm |
| MASS (WEIGHT) | METRIC TON<br>KILOGRAM* (KIL-uh-gram)<br>GRAM<br>MILLIGRAM | t<br>kg<br>g<br>mg | 1000 kg<br>1000 g<br>1000 mg |
| VOLUME OR CAPACITY | CUBIC METER*<br>LITER* (LEE-tur)<br>CUBIC CENTIMETER<br>MILLILITER | m³<br>L<br>cm³<br>mL | 1 m × 1 m × 1 m<br><br>= 1 mL |
| TIME | DAY HOUR<br>MINUTE<br>SECOND | d, h<br>min<br>s | |
| TEMPERATURE | DEGREE CELSIUS | °C | |

*Standards  These units are *standards* which are kept by the International Bureau of Weights and Measures in France. Note: The symbols are never followed by a period, except at the end of a sentence.

## Do and Discover

Investigation 5: What are the measurements of some common things?

### Procedures

1. Measure the mass (weight) of 10 paper clips. Use a gram scale.
2. Measure the mass (weight) of 22 sweet peas or 22 corn seeds.
3. Measure the perimeter (all four sides) of your *Pathways* book in cm.
4. Measure the water from 10 teaspoons into a small graduated cylinder.
5. Measure the water from 10 tablespoons into a graduated cylinder.
6. Measure the height of the door-opening in meters and centimeters.
7. Measure the mass of a liter of water. (Hint: The glass container also has mass.)

### Observations and Analysis

1. Record your figures in table form.
2. How much does one paper clip weigh?
3. How much does one seed weigh?
4. How many mL of cough medicine do you take in two teaspoons?

## SELF-STUDY GUIDE FOR CHAPTER 7

All answers should be written in your notebook. Please do not write in this book.

### Understanding the reading

A. *Find the Answers*
   Write the letter of the correct answer.
   1. What is the main idea of Chapter 7?
      a. Taking measurements requires a lab assistant.
      b. Measurements and notes are used by scientists for precise answers.
      c. There's no point taking notes if your measurements are not correct.
      d. Numbers and math are important for scientists.
   2. Numbers found by instruments are often arranged in such a way as
      a. to show results "at a glance."
      b. not to lose them.
      c. to be sure they are in metric style.
      d. to disprove incorrect theories.
   3. Scientists keep notes of their observations because
      a. they can review their observations later.
      b. it is a custom in science.
   c. notes explain diagrams.
   d. they need notes to prove they saw these things.
   4. Now that we have cameras, scientists
      a. never draw diagrams anymore.
      b. draw diagrams of plants only.
      c. draw diagrams and take photographs.
      d. draw diagrams only in laboratories.

B. *Locate the Idea*
   Find the sentence which answers each question. Write the sentence in your notebook.
   1. Section 7-7: How are the units in the metric system related to each other?
   2. Section 7-6: What do we call the basis for comparing measurements in all systems?
   3. Section 7-3: What method used by cooks may give *non-precise* measurements?
   4. Metric references, page 52: Where are the metric standards kept?

### Word tools

Complete the paragraph by choosing the correct words from the list. No word may be used more than once. (Two words will not be used.)

Sometimes we can guess or __(1)__ quantities. But scientists need more __(2)__ answers. There are many __(3)__ that measure mass, volume, and distance. Scientists always use the __(4)__ system of measurement. This system is based on the "tens" or __(5)__ idea. Very often large groups of numbers can be arranged in the form of tables or __(6)__.

estimate
metric
data
decimal
precise
units
graphs
gram

## Knowing what and why

A. *Number, Please . . .*
   In each group, state which is the *smallest* and which is the *largest*.
   1. meter, kilometer, centimeter
   2. hectare, $cm^2$, $km^2$
   3. kg, mg, g
   4. mL, $m^3$, L

B. *Do You Agree or Disagree?*
   Write a sentence stating your reasons.
   1. Measurements must have standards.
   2. The metric system is better than the English system.
   3. A tape recorder would be helpful to a scientist studying crickets.

C. *Understanding the Diagrams*
   Answer the questions with each graph.
   Look at the *circle graph*.
   1. *Without looking* at the numbers, which two elements are the least plentiful?
   2. Using the numbers, which is the *most* plentiful? The *least* plentiful?
   3. Invent a title for this graph.
   Now look at the *bar graph*.
   4. What is the major idea or "trend" of the past 80 years that this graph shows?
   5. Invent a title for the bar graph.

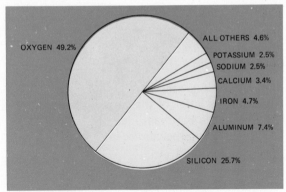

Fig. 54-1

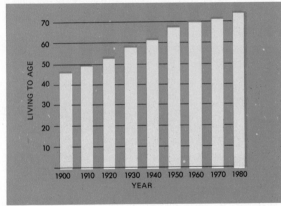

Fig. 54-2

## Looking further

1. Examine food packages at home. On each of ten labels find the mass ("weight"). What is your mass ("weight") in kg?
2. Measure the length and width of the doors in your house. Record your findings.
3. In what distances do track runners compete? (Hint: See *The World Almanac.*)
4. Make a circle graph showing the amount of time in a day and how you spend it. What activity takes most of your time?

# UNIT III

# When things are alive

## Unit III/outline

# When things are alive

## What's it all about?

"I slept like a rock last night," said Stephen. "I was dead to the world," said his friend Marjorie.

These are colorful ways of speaking, and we can be sure both friends had a good night's sleep. But you know, of course, that Stephen is not a rock because he is alive, and rocks are not alive. We know that when Marjorie slept, she stopped doing some of the things she does during the day. But, certainly she too was alive.

What does it mean to be *alive?* What does it mean *not* to be alive? There are certain signs of life which are clear to the senses. Other signs are not as clear.

Biologists speak of *life activities.* All life activities have one result: they keep the plant or animal living. When plants or animals stop these activities, they become ill or die.

In the last unit we learned that living things are part of their environment—both living and nonliving. Now we can go one step further. Living things must ADAPT (uh-DAPT) to their environment. ADAPTATION (ad-up-TAY-shun) means that the plant or animal makes itself *fit into* the environment. Life activities control adaptation.

In this unit, you will
- learn to recognize the signs of life.
- get an overall view of how living things function.
- understand how the activities of living things result in adaptation to the environment.

*And just as important,* you will
- discover how all life activities affect each other.
- observe and experiment to show what it means to be alive.

## chapter 8

**TARGET**     Is motion a sign of life?

# *Living things show action*

**Fig. 58-1**

Each of the pictures shows motion. Can you tell the difference in the kind of motion? Which of these things is alive?

## 8-1. Motion: a sign of life?

Have you ever watched someone who was asleep? Then you must have seen the person's chest move up and down. They probably changed their position many times. Perhaps they clenched their hands to make a fist. If a loose thread on the blanket tickled their ear, they brushed it away. When they felt cold, they pulled the blanket tightly around. When the alarm clock rang, perhaps they opened their eyes and then closed them. Finally, they got out of bed and the real world came back. They are fully awake.

Of course, rocks cannot do these things. And animals cannot do these things after they are dead.

## 8-2. Nonliving things show movement

Can a rock roll? Surely, but something must push it. Can a sailboat move? Yes, if the wind blows it. Can an automobile move? Of course, if its motor turns the wheels. Can a rocket enter space? Yes, if its jets blast it off the launching pad. In each case the nonliving thing must be moved by something.

## 8-3. Living things show movement

A fish can swim. A bird can fly. Humans can walk. These actions are controlled by the animals' bodies. A live geranium plant turns its leaves toward the light coming through a window. A live tree sends its roots toward a stream of water. A healthy ivy plant can spread its stems along a brick wall to a height of six or seven stories. These are examples of movement in plants and animals. How is the movement of a plant or animal different from the movement of a nonliving thing?

**Fig. 59-1**
**How can you prove that the leaves turn toward light?**

---

### Learned So Far . . .

- Motion is one sign of life.
- Living things, unlike nonliving things, provide their own movement.
- Plants, as well as animals, move.

---

## 8-4. Why all the motion?

All animals have a drive for survival. To stay alive, animals must be able to get food and get away from enemies. To carry on the species, animals must reproduce. Sometimes, an animal may have to fight for a mate. Or when the temperature drops, many animals move, or MIGRATE (MY-grayt), to a warmer climate. LOCOMOTION (loh-kuh-MOH-shun) is needed in each of these activities. It is an animal's "insurance policy" for staying alive.

Getting food may mean walking across a pasture as a cow does. It may mean swimming through the water like a shark.

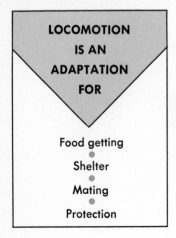

**LOCOMOTION IS AN ADAPTATION FOR**

Food getting
•
Shelter
•
Mating
•
Protection

Fig. 60-1

A gull flies through the air and nose-dives clear under water to come up with a fish dinner. A squirrel leaps from tree to tree collecting nuts. In each case an animal's locomotion is an adaptation to its environment.

Animals that eat meat must get food by capturing other animals. The fastest meat-eaters get food. The slowest starve. The fastest prey escape. The slowest die. Animals that eat grass must get to the area where the plants are growing. The salmon migrate over thousands of miles upstream to reproduce. Male frogs return to water to swim near the females for the act of mating. In many species, males fight furiously to win a mate. Later, the male fights to protect his mate and their young. Locomotion is a very important part of animal life.

### 8-5. Eagles and snails

He's "as slow as a snail!" She's "as fast as a rabbit!" Can't you just picture the people we are talking about?

Animals have many ways to move and they move with different speeds. The snail moves so slowly we can barely see it move. Slowly, it pushes along on a flap of muscle called a "foot." But it does get there! A deer can run at a speed of 70 km/h. An eagle flies at a speed of about 100 km/h. The fastest bird, a type of swift, has been clocked at around 170 km/h. The giant blue whale can swim at a speed of almost 40 km/h!

| HOW FAST DO THEY TRAVEL? | | | | | |
|---|---|---|---|---|---|
| Cheetah | 112 | Jackal | 56 | Squirrel | 19 |
| Lion | 80 | Rabbit | 56 | Chicken | 14 |
| Thomson's Gazelle | 80 | Giraffe | 51 | Giant Tortoise | 0.27 |
| Elk | 72 | Reindeer | 51 | Three-toed sloth | 0.24 |
| White-tailed deer | 72 | Cat, domestic | 48 | | |
| Coyote | 69 | Human | 44.6 | Garden Snail | 0.05 |
| Gray Fox | 68 | Elephant | 40 | | |

Note: Figures are in kilometers per hour (km/h). A car, driven at 55 miles per hour, is going at 88 km/h.

## 8-6. The moving parts

Animals move on land, in water, and through the air. The list on page 62 gives examples of organs of movement. Most microscopic animals float in water. All they need for movement is a line of hairs like oars. These are moved in rhythm. Others have one or two long "tails," which they lash to go ahead or in reverse. Starfish have hundreds of tube feet along the underside of their five arms. Movement is controlled by pumping water through the tube feet. The more complicated animals have either (or both) arms, legs, wings, fins, or tails.

Web (B)

A.

B.

C.

Fins (C)

D.

### Fig. 61-1

A bird's feet are adapted for walking, grasping, and fighting. Most birds have four toes, three in front, one behind (A).

A duck's feet have a web for swimming or wading (B).

Fins give a fish good control for swimming (C). How does the tail help?

Strong legs, arms, and tail help this "gymnast" (D).

| Animal | Organs of Movement |
|---|---|
| Microscopic animals | Hairs or "tails" |
| Starfish | Tube feet |
| Insects | Six legs; wings |
| Lobsters, spiders | Eight legs |
| Fish | Fins; tail |
| Snake | Body muscles and tail |
| Birds | Two rear legs; two front wings |
| Mammals | Four legs |

## Learned So Far . . .

- Living plants and animals often show some kind of action which we call movement, or locomotion.
- Living things move in order to carry on their life functions.

## SELF-STUDY GUIDE FOR CHAPTER 8

All answers should be written in your notebook. Please do not write in this book.

### Understanding the reading

A.  *Find the Answers*

Write the letter of the correct answer.
1. What is the main idea of Chapter 8?
   a. Movement is necessary for life functions.
   b. The fastest moving animals are the most successful.
   c. Living movement is more complicated than nonliving.
   d. After an animal is dead, it shows no movement.
2. What is the main idea of Section 8-1?
   a. Rocks cannot move.
   b. Movement means life.
   c. Breathing and tickling cause motion.
   d. Movement causes a change in position.

3. A duck moves with webbed feet and a beetle with six legs because
   a. each needs to breathe underwater.
   b. each moves only on land.
   c. each is adapted to its environment.
   d. locomotion is a sign of life.

B.  *Locate the Idea*

Find the sentence which answers each question. Write the sentence in your notebook.
1. Section 8-3: What motion is seen in an ivy plant?
2. Section 8-3: What causes a plant's leaves to turn?
3. Section 8-4: What is one cause for an animal's migration?
4. Section 8-4: Why do salmon migrate?

## Word tools

Match the animals from *Column A* with the correct organs or organs of movement from *Column B*. Use the chart on page 62. (One organ of movement will not be used.)

| Column A | Column B |
|---|---|
| 1. starfish | a. six legs |
| 2. spiders | b. tube feet |
| 3. fish | c. four legs |
| 4. birds | d. two rear legs; two front wings |
| 5. mammals | e. eight legs |
| | f. fins; tail |

## Knowing what and why

A.  *Do You Agree or Disagree?*

Write a sentence stating your reasons.
1. Plants as well as animals can move.
2. Locomotion is important in the struggle for existence. (Re-read Section 4-9.)
3. The fastest moving animal is the three-toed sloth.
4. Animals move only when they need to obtain food or a mate.

B.  *Puzzling It Out*

Answer these questions in a sentence or two.
1. A cat, 30 cm long, jumps to the top of a wall 150 cm high. If a 182-cm man could jump as high as a cat, how high could he jump?
2. Earthworms have no legs, wings, or fins. How do they move?
3. Why is it harder to run if you hold your arms stiffly at your sides?

C.  *Make a Chart*
1. Make a list of ten words which describe animal locomotion. For each word on your chart, write the name of an animal that shows that motion. Example: swim–shark.
2. See if you can name the *biome* each animal lives in and add it to your chart. (Look back to Chapter 4.)

## Looking further

1. Get a healthy plant that is growing in a pot. Place a chalk mark on one side of the pot. Place the plant on the window sill with the chalk mark facing the window. Leave it for a few days. What did the leaves do? Now turn the pot so that the chalk mark faces into the room. What happens after a few days? Write a report to give to the class.

2. Using a good almanac or an athletics handbook, look up the world speed record for track runners and long-distance swimmers. What are the physical characteristics of such athletes?

## chapter 9

TARGET    What do living things do when changes take place around them?

# *Living things respond to outside and inside changes*

**Fig. 64-1**

Can you explain what is happening in this picture?

### 9-1. Animals respond

When you whistle, your dog comes running to you. We say your dog RESPONDS to you. In other words, it answers your whistle. A response is like an answer. When a bright light is flashed in your eyes, your eyes respond by closing. When you smell food cooking in your kitchen, your mouth may respond by "watering." If your finger touches a hot pan, it responds by pulling away quickly.

### 9-2. Plants respond

You have seen the animal responses mentioned above many times. Since you know that plants are alive, you have probably guessed that they also respond. You are right! When there is a change around a plant, the plant responds. For example, if you water one side of a bush, the roots will grow toward the watered side. The leaves of a plant will actually grow around a wall to get light.

## Do and Discover

Investigation 6: How do plants respond to light?

**Procedures**
1. Set up the shoe box with a plant as shown.
   NOTE: The hole in the side is imaginary. It is
       just to show how it looks.
2. Water the plant daily.
3. Place the box so that the round opening faces
   toward the light.

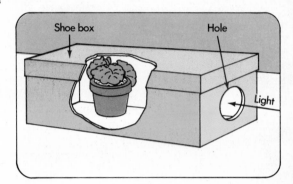

**Observations and Analysis**
1. Can you predict what will happen? Why?
2. Will colored light make a difference? (Hint:
   There are two ways to show this.)

**Fig. 65-1**

## Learned So Far . . .

● There are constant changes in the environment.
● Plants and animals show one or more responses to these changes.
  They do something.

### 9-3. The meaning of stimulus

Earlier, we saw that an alarm clock can wake a sleeping
person. The new sound is a change in the environment. Any
change in the environment is called a STIMULUS (STIM-
yuh-lus). The stimulus is received by the plant or animal.
The plant or animal then answers the stimulus with a response. Our SENSE ORGANS are used to receiving stimuli.

One STIMULUS; many STIM-
ULI (STIM-yuh-LY).

### 9-4. A stimulus brings on a response

When the heat in your environment changes, we say that the
temperature reading goes up or down. Your skin receives the
stimulus of heat and you may respond by taking off your
sweater. If it gets very hot, your skin may respond by sweating. If it gets very cold, your body may shiver and your skin
may show "goose pimples."

### 9-5. Some examples of responses

The chart shows some examples of animal responses to different stimuli. In each example, the stimulus–response pair is an adaptation that helps the animal to survive.

| Stimulus | Response |
|---|---|
| Bright light | eyes blink, animal may run away |
| Dim light | eye openings get wider |
| Loud sound | heavy breathing, animal jumps, runs |
| Soft sound | animal soothed, may doze |
| Rough, sharp, or hot | animal hurt—moans, screams |
| Object on skin | animal runs or fights |
| Good taste | animal licks lips, swallows, mouth waters |
| Bad taste | animal spits, runs away |

### 9-6. One response depends on another

You have probably been warned not to exercise too soon after eating. This is an example of how one system in your body causes changes in another system. In this case, the action of your muscles can affect your digestive system to give you cramps.

If you become very frightened, you may begin to run. Your muscles and skeleton begin to work hard. If you get angry, your heart begins to beat faster. Fear and anger are examples of our feelings, or EMOTIONS. Emotions can affect many of the systems of the body.

**Fig. 66-1**

A cat expresses fear by arching its back and raising its fur. In what other ways do animals show emotion?

## Do and Discover

Investigation 7: How do seeds respond to water?

### Procedures

1. Place six lima beans in each dish between layers of cotton.
2. Water the cotton in dish A every day for seven days. Leave dish B dry.

### Observations and Analysis

1. Make a chart to record your observations. Use it to write a brief description of what happened each day.
2. After you have your results, write a *conclusion* to your investigation.

3. Suppose several of your classmates challenge the conclusion you wrote.
   Make up an experiment to test each challenge.

   a. Jose: "Maybe the seeds in dish B are too old to germinate."

   b. Pamela: "It was too cold for the seeds to germinate."

   c. Joshua: "Why did you need dish B?"

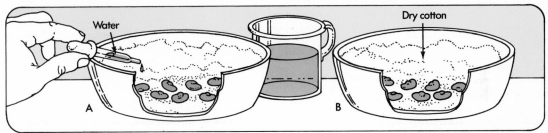

**Fig. 67-1**

## SELF-STUDY GUIDE FOR CHAPTER 9

All answers should be written in your notebook. Please do not write in this book.

### Understanding the reading

A.  *Find the Answers*
    Write the letter of the correct answer.
    1. What is the main idea of Chapter 9?
       a. Light is a stimulus for living things.
       b. A response is the action of a living thing.
       c. Living things respond to the environment.
       d. Emotions are stimuli.
    2. Dust in the nose makes a person sneeze because
       a. the dust is a stimulus.
       b. the dust is a response to breathing.
       c. sneezing is natural.
       d. sneezing is a form of rapid breathing.
    3. Some flowers close at night because
       a. it is cold.
       b. it is moist.
       c. it is dark.
       d. there is a lack of food.
    4. The stimulus to which we respond by shivering is usually the
       a. forming of "goose pimples."
       b. an increase in temperature.

c. a decrease in temperature.

d. an exercise to make us warmer.

B. *True or False*

If the statement is true, write *true*. If the statement is false, change the word in *italics* to make the statement true.

1. A change in the environment is a *response*.
2. Our *sense organs* receive stimuli.
3. Sneezing is a *stimulus*.
4. Fear and anger are *emotions*.
5. Shivering is a response to *heat*.
6. Responses are *harmful*.

## Word tools

Complete the paragraph by choosing the correct words from the list. No word may be used more than once. (Two words will not be used.)

When conditions in the __(1)__ change, living things must __(2)__ to the changed conditions. The change may come from plants or animals in the environment or from some __(3)__ factor. Whatever the cause, the change acts as a __(4)__ . The kinds of responses an animal makes shows how it has __(5)__ to its environment. The responses of human beings are made more complicated by their __(6)__ .

emotions
living
stimulus
respond
nonliving
locomotion
environment
adapted

## Knowing what and why

A. *Explanation, Please . . .*

Answer in one or two sentences.

1. An egg does not seem alive, but it hatches into a chick. What is the stimulus?
2. Skin, muscles, and bones may act as sense organs. Can you name one sensation (or stimulus) which is received by each of these three parts?
3. You walk into a dark room and it takes a while before you can see clearly.

B. *Make a Chart*

Look at the list in the next column. Which is a stimulus? Which is a response? Make a chart with two columns, one for *stimulus* and one for *response*. Write in all the stimuli from the list onto the chart. In the next column write a response that might result. Then write in all the responses from the list and think of a stimulus that could have caused each. Complete the chart.

1. the smell of laundry soap
2. a pistol shot
3. the downward growth of roots
4. bright headlights
5. trembling
6. a skunk's odor spray
7. a sunflower's movement toward the sun
8. a cat's attempt to scratch a dog
9. the stiffening of a rabbit's ears
10. the tickling of a baby's foot

## Looking further

1. Visit a local greenhouse. Ask the horticulturalist to tell you how the plants respond to light, temperature, and water. Write a report for your class.

2. Obtain a healthy geranium plant. Keep it in a dark box or closet for a few days. Water the plant daily. Observe the leaves. What stimulus caused this change?

## chapter 10

**TARGET    How do plants and animals take in food?**

# *Food is needed for life*

## 10-1. Feast, famine, and life

The newspaper clipping tells the sad story of a FAMINE (FAM-in), a period of great shortage of food for large numbers of people. The result is that many people actually starve to death. Even those who live become ill and weak. Fortunately, such things do not occur often in modern times. In fact, in some countries it is more common for people to eat *too much* and become overweight.

---

## WIDESPREAD FAMINE IN CAMBODIA FEARED

---

### Refugees' Tales Back Conclusions of Diplomats Who Study Area

---

**By HENRY KAMM**

Special to The New York Times

BANGKOK, Thailand, April 21—Widespread famine may be imminent in Cambodia, according to diplomats who follow events in Indochina.

Accounts, though sketchy, by refugees from the current fighting between the Vietnamese Army and Cambodian troops loyal to the ousted regime of Pol Pot lend support to the fears. The accounts tell of reduced rice crops and of people huddled for protection in towns where food stores have been removed or destroyed.

Officials here at the regional offices of the United Nations Food and Agriculture Organization and the World Food Program—the two international organizations likely to be involved in any relief effort—said they knew of no contingency plans at their headquarters and were making no plans at the regional level for an effort that would require long preparation.

The amount of food that is available often has to do with the land on which crops are grown. Farmers often judge soil as "rich" or "poor." What they really mean is how big or how plentiful the crop is that the soil produces.

These examples show that food has something to do with the health and the life of plants and animals. When there is plenty of the right kind of food, animals grow and stay healthy. When soil contains enough of the right kind of minerals, the plants grow tall and strong. In extreme cases, where there is no food at all, the plants and animals will die of starvation.

Getting food may seem like only one small life activity. It is not. It is a combination of many activities. Together, all the activities of plants and animals that have to do with getting and using food are called NUTRITION (new-TRISH-un).

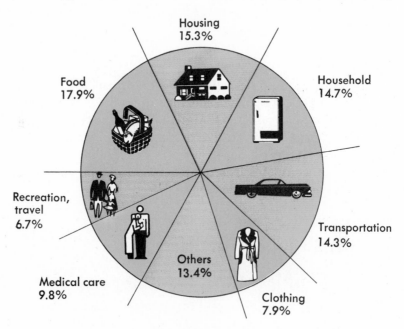

**Fig. 70-1**

Look at how much of our country's efforts deal with food! Might some of the other activities also deal with food? Explain.

## 10-2. What did you eat today?

You probably had food such as bread made from the wheat plant. Possibly you had a salad of lettuce and tomatoes. Of course, the wheat, lettuce, and tomatoes all grew from the soil. Perhaps you had eggs for breakfast. The hen that produced the eggs ate corn. Did you have fish for dinner? That fish probably ate smaller fish. But the smaller fish fed on ocean plants and animals. Did you eat steak from a cow, or lamb chops from a sheep? The cow and the sheep surely ate grass.

As you can see, all the foods you can think of can be traced back to green plants.

## 10-3. Patterns in food getting

In Chapter 4 you learned that green plants are *producers*. That is, only green plants can make their own food. But not only do green plants provide food for themselves, they feed other life as well. The nongreen plants and all animals live on materials made by green plants. Without green plants all life would quickly die.

## 10-4. Food for animals

Every animal has a way of getting food into its body. When we think of an animal eating, we usually think of a mouth. We know that most animals have some kind of mouth through which the food enters the body. In the more highly developed animals, hands, paws, or claws grasp the food and place it into the mouth. Many animals have sharp teeth and powerful jaws. These help them cut, rip, and grind the food into smaller bits before it is swallowed. The taking in of food is called INGESTION (in-JES-chun).

What do animals eat? The chart will give you an idea.

**Fig. 71-1**
How do human eating patterns differ from those of animals?

| | |
|---|---|
| **ANIMALS THAT EAT PLANT MATERIAL** | Birds: Fruits, Seeds<br>Horses: Oats<br>Squirrels: Nuts<br>Cattle: Grass |
| **ANIMALS THAT EAT FLESH** | Cats: Mice<br>Mountain Lions: Prairie Dogs<br>Sharks: Fish |
| **ANIMALS THAT EAT EVERYTHING** | Humans: Flesh and Plants |

### Learned So Far . . .

- The need for food is a sign of life.
- All food may be traced back to green plants.
- Animals have different ways of ingesting food.

### 10-5. How plants get food

Plants ABSORB (ab-SORB), or take in, water from the soil with their roots. "Good" soils have chemicals called MINERALS which help the plants grow. When plant roots absorb water, they also absorb any minerals which may be dissolved in the water. Sometimes we add minerals to the soil by using mixtures of chemicals called FERTILIZERS (FUR-tuhly-zurz). With the right amounts of water, minerals, and sunlight, green plants are able to manufacture their own food.

**Fig. 72-1**

**Plant roots absorb water and dissolved minerals through thin root hairs (left). Plants can be fed artificially by adding chemicals to the soil (right).**

### 10-6. Plants and animals without mouths

A tapeworm may reach a length of 6 meters. The beef tapeworm spends part of its life in the cow, the other part in humans.

There are some very simple animals which do *not* have mouths. An example of such an animal is the tapeworm which sometimes lives in the body of a human being. The tapeworm absorbs food right through its body wall. The bread mold plant which you grew at home and saw in the laboratory can absorb food directly from the bread.

There are also the insect-catching plants which live on live insects. The Venus's-flytrap is one such plant (see Figure 73-1).

## 10-7. Nutrition robbers

The bread mold lives on dead ORGANIC MATERIAL— something that was *once* alive. But the tapeworm lives in *living* things and robs them of food. So do the germs of tuberculosis and even athlete's foot. The *rust* that is seen on some wheat plants robs the wheat of its food. Such nutrition "robbers" are called PARASITES (PAR-uh-syts).

**Fig. 73-1**

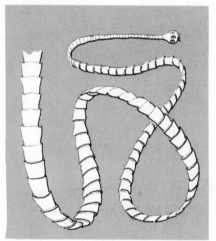 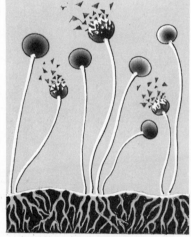

**Fig. 73-2**
Some animals (tapeworm, left) and plants (mold, right) absorb food. They do not ingest food.

## Learned So Far . . .

- Green plants make their own food.
- Some animals and plants take food from other living things.

## SELF-STUDY GUIDE FOR CHAPTER 10

All answers should be written in your notebook. Please do not write in this book.

*Understanding the reading*

A. *Find the Answers*
   Write the letter of the correct answer.
   1. Another title for Chapter 10 could be
      a. Even Simple Animals Use Food.
      b. Plants Make Their Own Food.
      c. Famines Around The World.
      d. Life Requires Food.

2. Plants usually get their food
   a. by absorbing it from soil directly.
   b. from fertilizers that are found in organic material.
   c. from other plants and animals.
   d. by absorbing minerals and water and then making food.
3. Which of these absorb food directly?
   a. Venus's-flytrap
   b. bread mold
   c. ants
   d. bees
4. About how much of United States industry deals with food?
   a. one fifth (1/5)
   b. one quarter (1/4)
   c. one half (1/2)
   d. two thirds (2/3)
5. Which animal uses green plants *directly* for food?
   a. mountain lion
   b. shark
   c. cat
   d. squirrel

B.  *Locate the Idea*
Find the section in which each of these questions is answered. Write the number of the section and one or two sentences that answer the question.
1. What materials in soil help plants grow best?
2. How does a tapeworm get food?
3. What do we call plant "food" that farmers add to soil?
4. Which plant eats insects?

C.  *Choose One*
Write the answer that correctly completes the sentence.
1. Plants (absorb, ingest) minerals through their roots.
2. A (tapeworm, Venus's-flytrap) is a parasite.
3. A shortage of food in the world is (an epidemic, a famine).
4. Green plants are the only organisms which are (parasites, producers).

## Word tools

Find the correct definition in *Column B* which describes the word in *Column A*. (One definition will not be used.)

**Column A**
1. producer
2. ingestion
3. parasite
4. famine
5. organic

**Column B**
a. food shortage
b. nutrition robber
c. flesh eater
d. green plant
e. taking in food
f. alive, or once alive

## Knowing what and why

A.  *Explanation, Please . . .*
Answer in one or two sentences.
1. How does chewing help animals to swallow food?
2. How are the tapeworm, tuberculosis germs, and wheat rust alike?

3. Why are some soils "richer" than others?

B.  *Do You Agree or Disagree?*
Write a sentence stating your reasons.
1. Famines never take place in modern times.

2. Minerals, when added to the soil, are absorbed into plant cells.
3. All life depends on green plants.
4. Parasites have a poor digestive system or none at all.

C. *On the Ladder of Understanding*
   Complete the statements. You may wish to review earlier chapters.

1. The common word *weight* refers to (volume, mass).
2. A glass bowl used to grow plants is called a(n) (terrarium, aquarium).
3. You would measure the length of your book in (meters, centimeters).
4. 1000 mL of milk will fill a (1 L, 10 L) container.

## Looking further

1. **Problem: Does fertilizer help plants grow?**
   Get a small amount of fertilizer and two healthy geranium plants. Add approximately 2 mL of the fertilizer to one of the plants once a week. Continue to water both plants with the same amount of water each day. Write a report of your results and bring it to class.

2. **Problem: How do plant stems carry water to the leaves?**
   Get a fresh stalk of celery. Cut the end off just about 3 cm from the bottom. Place it in a jar of water which you have colored with ink. Observe it for a few days. Write a report to explain what you observed and bring your report to class.

## chapter 11

**TARGET**     What is meant by digestion and circulation?

# *Food must be changed and delivered*

### 11-1. Making food ready for use

Have you ever heard of cooking food *twice?* This may sound silly, but it is what happens every time you eat a hamburger. The meat is cooked once before you eat it. Then, after you eat the hamburger, it is "cooked" a second time by your body. Your body "cooks" or makes ready for use all the food that you eat. This process of the body which makes food ready for use is called DIGESTION (dih-JES-chun).

### 11-2. What is digestion? Why is it necessary?

Earlier we said that some animals chop, grind, and cut food with their teeth. You will recall that these are methods which produce only physical changes. The MOLECULES (MOL-uh-kyoolz), or tiny particles, in the food remain the same. Foods contain many kinds of chemicals. Living things are able to use certain chemicals, but not others. To be able to get all the chemicals they need from foods, living things must have ways of changing the food *chemically* to simpler forms. *These chemical changes are a part of digestion.*

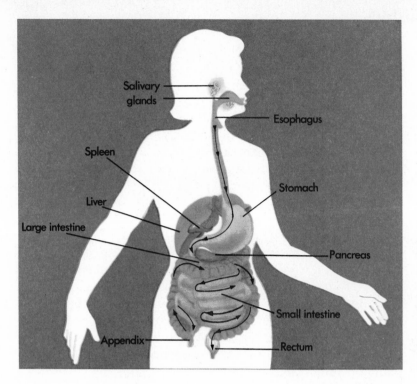

**Fig. 77-1**
Food is digested as it moves through most of the food tube. What is the advantage of a long digestive tube?

## Learned So Far . . .

- Digestion is a whole series of chemical changes.
- Plants and animals digest foods into simpler chemicals so that they can use them for life processes.

### 11-3. Where does digestion take place?

In most animals, including human beings, the digestive changes take place in a digestive CANAL or food canal. Examine the diagram of a human food canal. The food canal of a dog or cat is very similar to that of humans.

### 11-4. Digestive juices cause chemical changes in food

As the food moves through the food tube it is mixed and "bathed" in digestive juices. These chemicals are made in digestive GLANDS. The glands you know best are the SAL-IVARY (SAL-uh-ver-ee) GLANDS in the mouth which make a juice called SALIVA (suh-LY-vuh). You have surely felt this gland working when your mouth "waters." Actually, the saliva made by the glands is not just water. Dissolved in the water are chemicals which can cause chemical changes in certain foods that you eat.

## Learned So Far . . .

- Glands make chemical juices.
- These juices change food into simpler forms of chemicals in a food tube (canal).
- Digestion is a sign of life.

### 11-5. From head to foot

How long is a whale? Some whales are four times as long as your classroom. The whale's mouth is in its head, of course. But the food it eats must be able to reach every part of its body—even the muscles in its powerful tail fin, about 30 m away! How far is your big toe from your mouth? Yet your big toes and your ears and your brain must be fed. *All* parts of a plant or animal must be fed.

### 11-6. Delivering the finished product

You can see that it is not enough to digest food. It must also be moved or TRANSPORTED to all parts of the body. In many animals there is a system of branched tubes filled with a liquid called BLOOD. This blood moves around and around in a circular path through the whole body. We call this flow

**Fig. 78-1**

From mouth to feet, food must be first digested and then transported. A male giraffe may be over 5 meters tall. His neck may be over 2 meters long!

**Fig. 78-2**

The stream carries logs. The blood carries digested food.

of blood CIRCULATION (sur-kyuh-LAY-shun). Blood carries digested food to all parts of the body.

The blood in the blood tubes can be compared to the water in a river. Instead of logs, we can think of the small, simple molecules of digested food floating in the blood. This circulation carries the digested food molecules to parts of the body where they are needed—head, toes, brain, fingers—all parts.

### 11-7. Digestion and transport in plants

Green plants make their own food. But this food-making takes place in only certain parts. The manufactured food is transported by special tubes to all the other parts of the plant. Other tubes transport water and minerals as well.

When the food gets to the cells, it is digested by *each* cell. Plants do not have special digestive parts like animals.

### Learned So Far . . .

- Many animals have blood tubes in which blood circulates through their bodies.
- The blood carries dissolved and digested food molecules.
- Plants make food and transport it to all their parts.

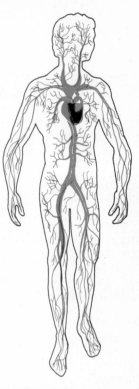

**Fig. 79-1**

The blood tubes carry digested food to all parts of the body. Why is this necessary?

## SELF-STUDY GUIDE FOR CHAPTER 11

All answers should be written in your notebook. Please do not write in this book.

*Understanding the reading*

A.  *Find the Answers*
    Write the letter of the correct answer.
    1. What is the main idea of Chapter 11?
       a. Your mouth waters when you smell food.
       b. Food is digested and then transported.
       c. Plants make their own food.
       d. Blood circulates throughout the whole body.

2. Digestion acts on food to
   a. change it into simple molecules.
   b. complete ingestion.
   c. change it to blood.
   d. move it to the stomach.
3. The glands in your mouth
   a. make saliva.
   b. cause physical changes in food.
   c. give you an appetite.
   d. make taste possible.

4. Eating and chewing do *not* cause digestion because
    a. they take too short a time.
    b. the food does not go far.
    c. these are physical changes.
    d. these are chemical changes.

B. *Locate the Idea*
Find the section in which each of these questions is answered. Write the number of the section and one or two sentences that answer the question.

1. What juice is in your mouth when it "waters"?
2. What tube carries food from the mouth to the stomach?
3. What liquid transports digested food in animals?
4. What structures transport food in plants?
5. What glands supply the mouth with digestive juice?

## Word tools

Unscramble the groups of letters in *Column A* to form science words. Then match them with their correct definitions from *Column B*.

**Column A**
1. ZFETRILIRE
2. OTGIDIESN
3. ONIGSTIEN
4. DLNAG
5. ALSIVA

**Column B**
a. eating
b. chemical change of food
c. digestive juice from the mouth
d. food for plants
e. "factory" for digestive juices

## Knowing what and why

A. *Explanation, Please . . .*
Answer in one or two sentences.
1. How is your food "cooked" twice?
2. Is chewing a chemical or physical change?
3. How are digestion and circulation related?
4. How is digestion in plants *different* from digestion in animals?

B. *On the Ladder of Understanding*
Complete the statements. You may wish to review earlier chapters.
1. Insects have _____ legs, while spiders have _____.
2. Human body temperature is usually _____ degrees Celsius.
3. There are _____ meters in 4 kilometers.

## Looking further

Interview your family doctor. Does he or she use a FLUOROSCOPE (FLOOR-uh-skohp)? Have the doctor explain its use to you.

## chapter 12

**TARGET**    Why is breathing a sign of life? What wastes are formed by living things?

# *Using the food-getting rid of the wastes*

### 12-1. "Is he still breathing?"

This is the most common question asked when we want to know whether someone is alive. It is easy to see your parakeet, your puppy or your friend breathing. You can see his chest grow larger and smaller, as he takes in air and gives out air. We call this BREATHING. The pictures show how different living things breathe.

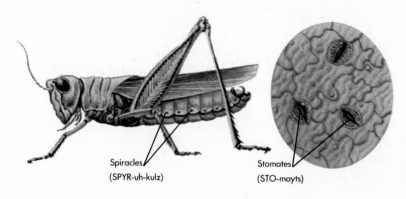

Spiracles
(SPYR-uh-kulz)

Stomates
(STO-mayts)

**Fig. 81-1**
Insects breathe through openings on the side of their bodies called *spiracles*. Plants breathe through *stomates* on the underside of their leaves.

### 12-2. How are wastes formed?

In a coal furnace, part of the fuel cannot burn. It is left over as a waste, called *ashes*. When animals eat food, some solid parts are not digested. This is left as semi-solid waste. Water is also left over as a waste.

### 12-3. Wastes released by breathing

Chemists know that carbon dioxide forms if you burn materials containing carbon. This is called OXIDATION (ok-sih-DAY-shun). The chemical compounds that make up food contain carbon. You breathe out carbon dioxide. Look at the diagram.

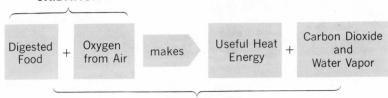

**OXIDATION**

| Digested Food | + | Oxygen from Air | makes | Useful Heat Energy | + | Carbon Dioxide and Water Vapor |

**RESPIRATION**

The oxidation of food is called RESPIRATION (res-puh-RAY-shun). The two wastes formed in respiration are two gases you have studied before: *carbon dioxide* and *water vapor*.

### 12-4. "Wow, was I sweating!"

How often you have heard this remark after coming out of the gym! Of course, the harder you play, the more energy you need, and the more food you "burn" through oxidation. You breathe faster and your skin gives off SWEAT. Another name for sweat is PERSPIRATION (pur-spuh-RAY-shun). Perspiration is a mixture of water, salt, and other wastes. Sweating is one way your body gives off waste.

### 12-5. Getting rid of wastes

In living things all life actions produce wastes. These wastes must be removed from the body of the plant or animal to keep it working smoothly and in good health. The removal of

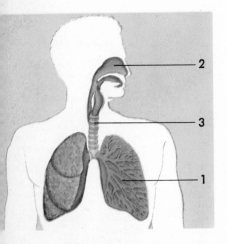

**Fig. 82-1**

We breathe to obtain air and its oxygen. Can you name the numbered parts?

wastes from living things is called EXCRETION (ik-SKREE-shun).

In many animals, blood helps to carry waste from different parts of the body to the organs of excretion.

## 12-6. Water means life

One of the greatest fears of lost people is that they will die of thirst. The shipwrecked sailor on a lonely island, the flyer forced down in the desert, the people on rafts and lifeboats all search for the same "treasure"—water! Why? All land animals must have a balance of water taken in and water given off. The amount of water in the body is regulated in two ways:

**1. By urination:** Urine is formed in the KIDNEYS (KID-neez) from water in the blood. The urine is stored in the BLADDER.

**2. By sweating:** Sweat is released through the pores of the skin.

If too much water is lost, the body becomes DEHY-DRATED (dee-HY-drayt-ed). Cramps and weakness are early signs. Unless water is taken in, death soon results.

Blow your breath out onto a mirror. You can see the water vapor condense to form tiny droplets of water.

## Do and Discover

Investigation 8: How much sweat is given off by the skin?

### Procedures

1. Place your thumb inside a dry, 50 mL graduated cylinder. Seal the top around your finger with adhesive tape. Keep it on for thirty minutes while you sit *quietly* reading or watching TV.
2. Remove the graduated cylinder from your finger. Read the volume of sweat.
3. Repeat the experiment but this time exercise vigorously for about ten minutes while you collect the sweat.

### Observations and Analysis

1. How many milliliters (mL) are formed in step 2? In step 3?
2. Explain why different amounts of sweat formed.

3. Would smearing grease or cold cream on your thumb make a difference? Explain.
4. How could you collect sweat from your entire arm?

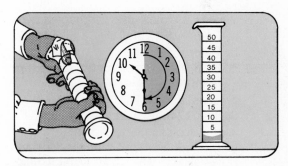

Fig. 83-1

## THE KINDS OF WASTES

| Waste | What It Is |
|---|---|
| Solid waste | Undigested solids |
| Perspiration (sweat) | Water, salt, and urea |
| Urine | Water, salt, and urea |
| Exhaled air | Carbon dioxide and water vapor |

## Learned So Far . . .

- Living things need oxygen for respiration.
- Living things form wastes after using food.
- Respiration is a sign of life.
- Excretion is a sign of life.

## SELF-STUDY GUIDE FOR CHAPTER 12

All answers should be written in your notebook. Please do not write in this book.

### Understanding the reading

A. *Find the Answers*

Write the letter of the correct answer.

1. What is the main idea of Chapter 12?
   a. Even insects and plants take in air.
   b. Water means life.
   c. Food is oxidized and wastes are given off.
   d. Sweating is a form of waste.
2. Section 12-6 explains
   a. that food contains carbon.
   b. that urine is stored in the kidneys.
   c. the ways in which body water is regulated.
   d. the causes of cramps.
3. Exercise causes faster breathing and results in more
   a. oxidation.
   b. ingestion.
   c. dehydration.
   d. digestion.
4. Oxygen is removed from the air in the
   a. windpipe.
   b. throat.
   c. stomates.
   d. lungs.
5. The waste products of *respiration* are
   a. carbon dioxide and urea.
   b. carbon dioxide and water vapor.
   c. water vapor and urea.
   d. salt and water vapor.

## Word tools

Complete the paragraph by choosing the correct words from the list. No word is used more than once. (Two words will not be used.)

| |
|---|
| breathing |
| nitrogen |
| oxygen |
| water vapor |
| oxidize |
| spiracles |
| windpipe |
| carbon dioxide |
| stomates |
| nostrils |

To get energy from food, we must __(1)__ it. We take in air by __(2)__ and then remove the useful element, __(3)__ . The wastes formed in this process are __(4)__ and __(5)__ . If I were a grasshopper I would breathe with __(6)__ . Since I am human, I breathe through my __(7)__ and send air to my lungs through my __(8)__ .

## Knowing what and why

A. *Puzzling It Out*
   Answer these questions in a sentence or two.
   1. Why are rubber gloves often uncomfortable?

   2. Why should cold creams and other cosmetics be washed off the face before going to sleep?
   3. Why do travelers in the desert urinate very little?

## Looking further

Try this experiment on your own.
**Problem: What is the cooling action of the skin?**
**Procedures**
1. Prepare two wads of absorbent cotton. Dip the first in water. Write your name on the chalkboard. Then wet your arm with the wet cotton.
2. Repeat these actions with cotton soaked in alcohol.

**Observations and Analysis**
1. Which evaporates faster—water or alcohol?
2. Which piece of cotton cools more?
3. What purpose does writing on the chalkboard serve?
4. Why is alcohol used to sponge the body of a patient with fever?

## chapter 13

TARGET    How is growth a sign of life?

# Growing and living

**Fig. 86-1**

How long will it be before the baby is too heavy to carry? How long before it reaches the mass of its father?

### 13-1. Big and little—old and young

Have you ever seen a picture of yourself when you were a baby? How much did you weigh? Do you remember your dog when it was a small pup? Can you remember the big tree on your street when it was first planted? What has happened to it since then? Aren't you amazed when you find that your clothes from last year are a couple of sizes too small? How does this all happen?

### 13-2. Growth is a sign of life

We see many examples of growth all around us. One haircut in your life is not enough. You may need hundreds. Cutting your nails once is not enough. You must cut your nails quite often. Many men shave 365 times a year! Do you worry about the peeling skin on your sunburnt back? Of course not! You know that you will grow new skin very soon. Last week's cut finger is soon healed. After a short period, new flesh and new skin appear. Last year's broken wrist is only a memory. The broken ends of the bone were mended with new bone and your wrist is as good as before. The hedges you pruned (cut) last week have grown back again and need another cutting.

All of these are examples of the wonderful life process called GROWTH.

86

## Learned So Far . . .

- All living things show some kind of growth.
- Growth is a sign of life.

### 13-3. Digested food into living matter

You have already learned that living things can form new skin, new bones, new leaves, new stems. It follows that this new material must be made from something. New living matter comes from digested food. Living things are able to cause chemical changes in the molecules of the digested food so that the food becomes part of their own bodies.

| THE OLD AND THE YOUNG | |
|---|---|
| **Adults** | **Young** |
| dogs, seals | pups |
| cats, leopards | kittens |
| bears, lions | cubs |
| geese | goslings |
| ducks | ducklings |
| deer | fawns |
| fish | fry |
| cattle, elephant, whale | calves |
| sheep | lamb |
| horse | colt, foal |
| pig | piglet |
| plant | seedling |
| tree | sapling |

Fig. 87-1

What factors control the growth of the young? In each group, how do the parents contribute to the growth of their young?

### 13-4. Chemicals into living matter

Chemists have studied what makes up living matter. One kind of compound found in living things but not in nonliving things is called PROTEINS (PROH-teenz). Our bodies also contain other chemicals. For example, our blood is rich in the element IRON. Our bones are rich in CALCIUM.

The living process by which plants and animals change food into living matter is called ASSIMILATION (uh-sim-uh-LAY-shun). During assimilation, digested food turns into living matter for growth and repair.

## Learned So Far . . .

- Digested food is turned into living matter by assimilation.
- Growth is possible because of assimilation.
- The process of assimilation repairs broken and damaged parts.
- Assimilation is a sign of life.

### 13-5. Plants show growth

Look back to Chapter 3. You saw that plant cuttings can grow new roots. Tomatoes, apples, and corn are small in the early part of the season. As they assimilate sugar, starch, and protein, they grow bigger. Trees grow from tiny saplings to huge trees 10, 15, or 30 meters tall. Once again, food is changed by assimilation into proteins and other chemicals. Plants store food in their roots, stems, and leaves. Tree trunks store special materials to form wood and bark. Trunks grow tall and give out many branches. Their leaves grow large. Growth is a life function of all plants.

### 13-6. Reaching for the sky

Tall, woody trees are nature's largest living things. They reach high into the sky and show enormous girth (distance around the trunk). In almost every community you can see examples. The chart lists some of the greatest.

**Fig. 88-1**

These trees found near Yosemite Falls were once saplings. Assimilation of food made them tall and thick. Explain how.

Many tall trees have a girth from 2 to 4.5 meters. The Coast Redwood has a girth of 13.2 meters.

| TALLEST TREES OF THE U.S. | | |
|---|---|---|
| **Trees** | **Location** | **Height in Meters** |
| Beech, American | Three Oaks, Mich. | 48.6 |
| Buckeye, Painted | Union County, Ga. | 43.2 |
| Cedar, Port Oxford | Siskiyou National Park, Ore. | 65.7 |
| Douglas Fir | Coos Bay, Oregon | 90.6 |
| Hemlock, Western | Olympic National Park, Wash. | 48.0 |
| Pine, Ponderosa | Plumas, Calif. | 67.0 |
| Redwood, Coast | Humboldt State Park, Calif. | 108.6 |
| Sequoia, Giant | Sequoia National Park, Calif. | 81.6 |
| Spruce, Sitka | Seaside, Oregon | 64.8 |

### 13-7. Living longer

Unless disease, famine, or disasters such as forest fires or volcanoes destroy living things, populations keep increasing. With human beings and livestock (cows, sheep, chickens), we have found ways to stop disease and protect the young. Therefore, humans and livestock live longer lives than they used to. We say we have increased LONGEVITY (lon-JEV-ih-tee). Study the graph. Can you tell what has happened to the longevity of humans in the last 80 years?

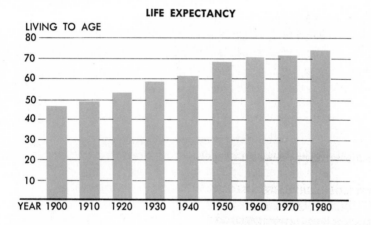

**LIFE EXPECTANCY**

**Fig. 89-1**

Life expectancy in the U.S. What does the graph show? How much has life expectancy increased between 1910 and 1980?

### Learned So Far . . .

- Some plants can grow to enormous sizes.
- Humans live longer now than ever before.

## SELF-STUDY GUIDE FOR CHAPTER 13

All answers should be written in your notebook. Please do not write in this book.

### Understanding the reading

A. *Find the Answers*
Write the letter of the correct answer.
1. Which of the following ideas is *not* discussed in this chapter?
   a. Animals gain mass as they grow older.
   b. Growth is a sign of life.
   c. Food is changed to living matter.
   d. Without minerals there is no growth.
2. Proteins are chemical compounds which
   a. cause oxidation.
   b. are found only in living things.
   c. are waste products after respiration.
   d. are similar to carbon dioxide.
3. Growth is a life activity that depends on the assimilation of

a. sunlight.
b. urea.
c. food.
d. ingestion.
4. If two plants are growing in the same soil and get the same amount of light and water, we can speed up the growth of one of them by adding
a. carbon dioxide.
b. oxygen.
c. urea.
d. fertilizer.

B. Which One?
In the following groups of words find the "umbrella" word: the one word which *includes* the other three.
Example: penny, coin, dime, nickel: *coin*
1. ingestion, digestion, nutrition, assimilation
2. respiration, oxidation, breathing, exhaling
3. urine, perspiration, carbon dioxide, excretion
4. nutrition, parasite, consumer, producer

## Word tools

Find the correct definition from *Column B* which describes the word in *Column A*. (One definition will not be used.)

**Column A**

1. iron
2. protein
3. longevity
4. assimilation
5. calcium

**Column B**

a. element necessary for oxidation
b. important element in blood
c. compound of living things
d. process of food becoming living matter
e. necessary for bone growth
f. length of life

## Knowing what and why

A. Explanation, Please . . .
Answer in one or two sentences.
1. What process changes food to flesh and bone?
2. What chemical is needed to form bones?
3. How does a tree trunk grow thick?

B. Understanding the Graph
Look back to the graph on life expectancy, Figure 89-1.
1. Was the increase in life expectancy the same every ten years?

2. How do you think this graph would compare to that of a developing country in Asia or Africa? Explain.
3. How do you think the graph will look in the year 2000?
4. Does this graph show differences in life expectancy between black and white people? Between men and women? Do you think there may be a difference? Why?

## Looking further

Write to the World Health Organization, United Nations, New York, N.Y. 10017. Ask for booklets about feeding the people in developing nations. Write a report for your class.

## chapter 14

**TARGET**     How do plants and animals "live forever"?

# *Living things produce new generations*

## 14-1. The next generation

Not only do living things grow large; they also grow old. And of course you know that sooner or later living things die. And yet there are always new plants and animals. As a matter of fact, we know that there are more plants and animals today than at the time of Columbus or Washington. The reason is that living things produce young. We sometimes say that plants and animals "give birth." This process is called REPRODUCTION (ree-pruh-DUK-shun). Plants and animals leave a new generation. In this way they "live forever."

## 14-2. Population grows

Experts predict that in forty years the human population of the world will *double*. As you know, when a dog has a litter of puppies, it is usually not just two puppies. In other words, the father and mother are not just replaced. Generally, a litter consists of many puppies. This is true of human beings too. Although only one child is usually born at a time, many

Fig. 91-1
Zebras and their young.

91

families have *twins* (two), *triplets* (three), or even QUAD-RUPLETS (four). There are even rare cases of QUINTU-PLETS (five)!

### 14-3. Reproduction in stages

Have you heard of the TADPOLE, a tiny creature that lives in water in the spring? Did you know that a baby tadpole does not grow up to be an adult tadpole, but a frog? This is a special kind of growth, in which the young look very different from the old.

Another example is the crawling CATERPILLAR, with fuzzy body and many legs, which grows to be a beautiful butterfly or moth with wings.

**Fig. 92-1**

Some living things look very different when they are young. The painted lady butterfly is a good example.

### 14-4. Reproduction with seeds

Did you know that a handful of corn seeds, properly planted, can grow hundreds of ears of corn? Did you know that the Pilgrims brought seeds of wheat to Plymouth to plant new crops? Seeds are made by plants for reproduction. Apple seeds grow into apple trees. Pumpkin seeds grow into pumpkins.

**Fig. 92-2**

Seeds grow into plants. Look back to Figure 72-1. How are those pictures related to this picture?

## 14-5. Reproduction with spores

In Chapter 3 we saw how mold can grow on bread. The living mold "shoots out" tiny, invisible SPORES. When other spores land on bread, jelly, cheese, or fruit, they grow to be a new mold. By keeping food covered, we keep the spores away and stop food from spoiling.

**Fig. 93-1**
Mushrooms also reproduce by spores. The spores fall onto the soil and grow new mushrooms.

## 14-6. Reproduction with eggs and sperm

Many plants and animals have two sexes, male and female. Male animals produce SPERM and female animals produce EGGS. When a sperm and an egg combine, the new bit of living matter grows into a new living thing. This kind of reproduction is called SEXUAL REPRODUCTION.

## 14-7. The needs of living things

The basic need of living things is to continue to live and produce a new generation. The chart on page 94 shows these needs and how they are related to life activities.

## Learned So Far . . .

- Living things reproduce young like themselves.
- Reproduction is a sign of life.

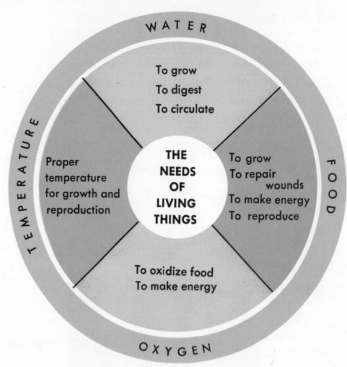

Fig. 94-1

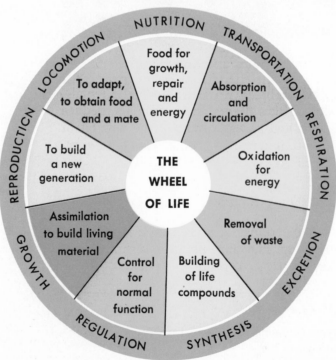

Fig. 94-2

## SELF-STUDY GUIDE FOR CHAPTER 14

All answers should be written in your notebook. Please do not write in this book.

### Understanding the reading

A. *Find the Answers*

Write the letter of the correct answer.
1. Another title for Chapter 14 could be
   a. Molds, Spores, and Seeds.
   b. The Next Generation.
   c. The Wheel of Life.
   d. The Needs of Living Things.
2. Sexual reproduction requires
   a. seeds and spores.
   b. assimilation and longevity.
   c. growth and oxidation.
   d. sperm and eggs
3. Tadpoles are to frogs as caterpillars are to
   a. forests.
   b. ponds.
   c. butterflies.
   d. molds.
4. Section 14-3 explains that
   a. molds reproduce by spores.
   b. dogs and cats reproduce sexually.
   c. tomatoes reproduce by seeds.
   d. tadpoles become frogs.

B. *True or False*

If the statement is true, write *true*. If the statement is false, change the word in *italics* to make the statement true.
1. Molds reproduce by *seeds*.
2. A moth was once a *tadpole*.
3. The life function that creates a new generation is *reproduction*.
4. Males produce *eggs*.

### Word tools

In your notebook, draw the blanks as shown. Fill in the words that match the definition. The first letters, read downward, spell something you eat.

1. To take in air
2. To produce young
3. To give off waste
4. To change food to living matter
5. To break food into simple molecules

1. ⬜ — — — — — —
2. ⬜ — — — — — — — —
3. ⬜ — — — — — —
4. ⬜ — — — — — — — —
5. ⬜ — — — — —

### Knowing what and why

A. *In Your Own Words*
For each of the four words below write a single sentence using the word and giving its meaning.
1. longevity
2. sperm
3. caterpillar
4. tadpole

B. *Puzzling It Out*
Answer this question in a sentence or two. Life expectancy for American black males born in 1976 will be 64.1 years. White males born the same year have a 69.7 year life expectancy. How can you explain this?

C. *On the Ladder of Understanding*
Use the correct words from the list to complete each sentence. (Two words will not be used.)
You may wish to review earlier chapters.

1. Perspiration is an example of _____.
2. Spores are a part of the process known as _____.
3. Oxygen is necessary to carry on _____.
4. The body prepares food for use by the process known as _____.
5. Growth is made possible by _____.
6. Blood is carried to all parts of the body by _____.
7. Eating is _____.

digestion
respiration
assimilation
reproduction
circulation
excretion
ingestion
longevity
saliva

## Looking further

1. In the *Information Please Almanac* (in your library) look up GESTATION (jeh-STAY-shun) of animals. This is the period of growth of an animal in its mother's body. Make a list of the most common animals and their gestation periods.

2. Mushroom spores can be examined easily. Pick mushrooms and place the caps on colored construction paper. The spores will be released as the mushrooms dry. You can preserve the spore prints they leave by spraying with hair spray.

# UNIT IV

# *The building blocks of living things*

## Unit IV/outline

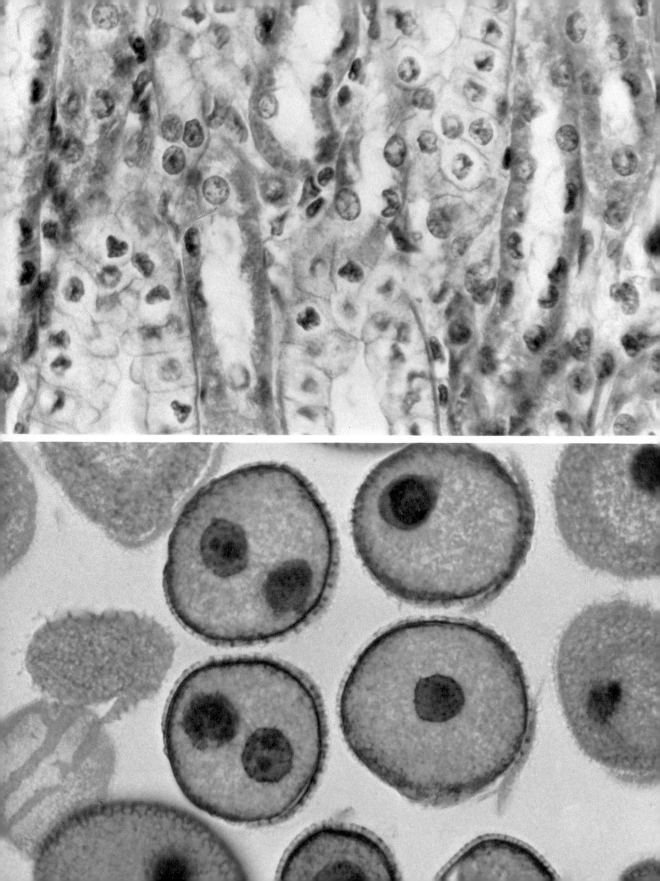

# The building blocks of living things

## What's it all about?

"Let's take a closer look!"

How often have we heard this expression? We see things. We want to see them better. We want to understand how they work. This is how scientists felt long ago when they began studying living things.

Hundreds of questions raced through their minds: What makes a muscle move? Why does the eye "see"? Why is bone hard? Why are leaves green and blood red? Of what is "living stuff" made?

Before such questions could be answered, scientists had to get a closer look at the "living stuff." Their eyes could see only the surface. The search began with the invention of the MICROSCOPE.

A new world was opened! Scientists could now look *below* the surface of skin, muscle, and leaves. They could even look into a new world—the world of life previously unseen by the naked eye.

In this unit, you will learn
- how a microscope works.
- what living things look like under a microscope.
- about the building blocks of plants and animals.
- about tiny forms of life, visible only with the use of a microscope.

*And, just as important,* you will
- learn to use a microscope.
- find out how to examine living material.
- understand how living parts form a "team" for life activities.

## chapter 15

# The microscope— wonderful tool of science

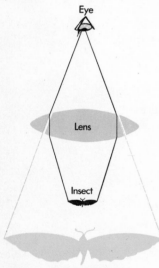

Eye

Lens

Insect

Enlarged image

## Fig. 100-1

Although one of the simplest of the scientist's tools, the magnifying glass is one of the most important tools. Why would this be true?

### 15-1. When things are smaller than the eye can see

Have you ever seen a person repair a watch? When looking inside a watch, a MAGNIFYING GLASS is usually placed in front of the eye. A LENS, which is a specially prepared piece of glass, then magnifies, or enlarges, the tiny wheels in the watch. Such lenses were invented by the ancient Chinese people. The simplest lens, shown in Fig. 100-1, is a single glass lens. You can use it to examine the wings of an insect, the pores in your skin, or the inner parts of a flower. Also, you can enlarge a whole animal, such as a tiny flea or a termite.

A lens is really a simple MICROSCOPE. *Micro* means small. *Scope* means to see. A microscope is an instrument used to see small objects.

### 15-2. Two lenses are better than one

Suppose you wanted to enlarge the image of an object even more than you could with one lens. Scientists long ago found a very simple way. They used two lenses, placing one behind the other inside a tube. See Figure 101-1.

## Learned So Far . . .

- A lens is a specially prepared piece of glass that can magnify small objects.
- Two lenses placed one behind the other can give greater magnification than one lens alone.

### 15-3. The idea of the compound microscope

A microscope that combines two lenses is called a COMPOUND MICROSCOPE. It is easy to figure out *how much* a microscope can magnify by multiplying the power of one lens by the power of the other. For example, suppose Lens B in Figure 101-1 magnifies *five* times (5x) and Lens D magnifies this image *ten* times (10x). We then multiply the power of Lens B by the power of Lens D. The Image E which we see is enlarged 5 times 10, or 50 times. Many school microscopes have lenses that enlarge 10x with the first lens and 10x with the second lens. Your eye will then see the object 10 times 10 or 100 times as large as its true size.

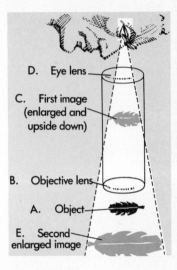

D. Eye lens

C. First image (enlarged and upside down)

B. Objective lens

A. Object

E. Second enlarged image

**Fig. 101-1**

This diagram shows how a *compound* microscope works. Why do you think it is called compound? Explain how it works.

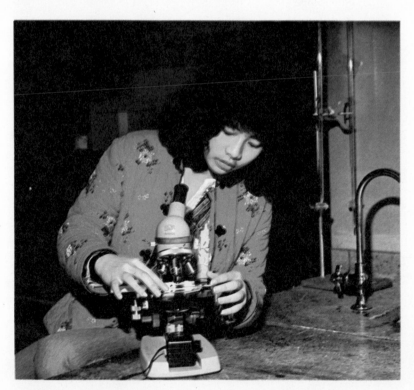

**Fig. 101-2**

The modern microscope is a big improvement over those made long ago.

## 15-4. Knowing the parts of your microscope

The microscope shown in Figure 101-2 is a compound microscope. It is probably like the ones in your school. The microscope is a valuable and delicate instrument. *It must be handled with care.* Do you know how to use it properly?

If you wanted to learn how to drive a car, you would first learn the names of the controls and the job of each part. To use a microscope correctly, you should know the parts of the microscope and their jobs. Look at Figure 102-1 to learn the names of the parts. Study them. Then your teacher will instruct you how to use the microscope correctly.

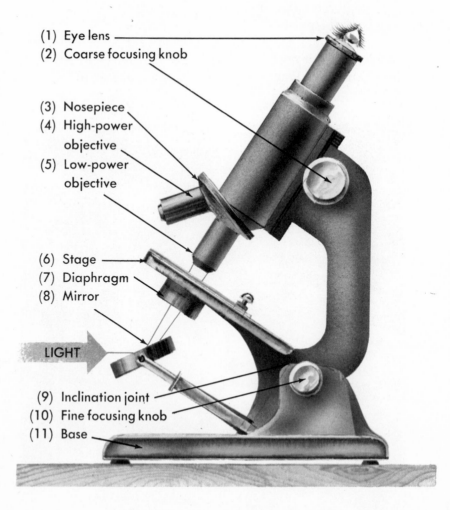

(1) Eye lens
(2) Coarse focusing knob

(3) Nosepiece
(4) High-power objective
(5) Low-power objective

(6) Stage
(7) Diaphragm
(8) Mirror

LIGHT

(9) Inclination joint
(10) Fine focusing knob
(11) Base

**Fig. 102-1**

A compound microscope. Look at the parts and tell what each is used for.

## 15-5. Preparing the object to be viewed

Objects to be viewed under a microscope must be very thin. The reason for this is that enough light must pass *through* the object and *through* the lenses to reach your eye. Objects which allow some light to go through them are said to be TRANSLUCENT (trans-LOO-sunt). Frosted glass and wax paper are examples of translucent materials. Parts of living things must be peeled very thin to make them translucent. For example, you cannot view a whole leaf under the microscope. You must peel off a very thin layer. Objects to be viewed are placed on a glass *slide,* usually in a drop of water. The drop is then covered with a thin plastic or glass cover. Next the slide is placed on the stage over the hole in its center. In this way light can shine through the slide.

## 15-6. Learning to use the microscope

After the slide is on the stage, you must lower the clips to hold the slide in place. You can swing either the low-power lens or the high-power lens into place. Either way, the objective lens must be in line with the eye lens. The mirror is placed in such a way that light passes through the hole, through the slide, and then through the object. The two sets of adjustment knobs help you to FOCUS (FOH-kus), or make the image clear. You focus by turning the knobs *toward* you. This action *raises* the tube. When the tube is raised the correct distance, the image comes into focus.

Now you're ready to look at the real thing. The investigation that follows shows how *you* can use the microscope to study a part of your own body. In the next few chapters we will take an even closer look at the "inside story" of living things.

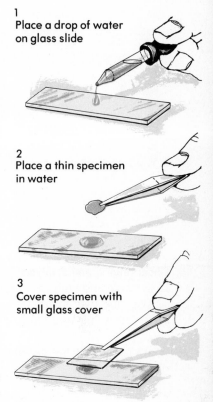

1 Place a drop of water on glass slide

2 Place a thin specimen in water

3 Cover specimen with small glass cover

**Fig. 103-1**

This diagram shows the three steps needed to make a slide. Remember the objects placed in the water (step 2) must be translucent.

The powerful ELECTRON MICROSCOPE uses electrons to form an image on a fluorescent screen.

## Learned So Far . . .

- Objects to be viewed with a microscope must be translucent.
- The mirror on a microscope directs light through the object being viewed.
- The knobs on a microscope help you focus for a clear image.

## Do and Discover

Investigation 9: How can we observe cheek tissue under the microscope?

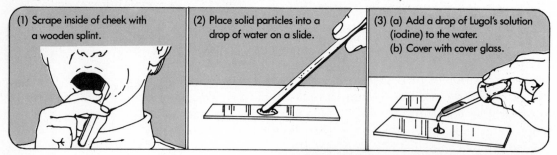

(1) Scrape inside of cheek with a wooden splint.

(2) Place solid particles into a drop of water on a slide.

(3) (a) Add a drop of Lugol's solution (iodine) to the water.
(b) Cover with cover glass.

**Procedures**
Follow steps 1 through 3 as shown in the diagrams.

**Observations and Analysis**
1. Observe and study the cells (steps 4 and 5). Describe their shape.
2. Is yellow the true color of cheek tissue? Explain.
3. Which part of the cell looks darker? Why?

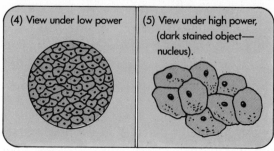

(4) View under low power

(5) View under high power, (dark stained object— nucleus).

**Fig. 104-1**

## SELF-STUDY GUIDE FOR CHAPTER 15

All answers should be written in your notebook. Please do not write in this book.

*Understanding the reading* _____

A.  *Find the Answers*
Write the letter of the correct answer.
1. What is the main idea of Chapter 15?
    a. A physician must have a microscope.
    b. A biologist must have a microscope.
    c. Microscopes magnify living material.
    d. A microscope can view only very thin tissue.
2. You cannot use all three lenses on the student microscope (Figure 101-2) because

a. you can line up only two of them at one time.
b. one lens is too weak.
c. the lenses don't match.
d. the mirror does not work this way.
3. The simple magnifying glass would be *least* useful to examine
    a. bread mold.
    b. the inside of a plant's stem.
    c. a mosquito's eye.
    d. a bee's leg.

B. *Locate the Idea*
Find the section in which each of these questions is answered. Write the number of the section and one or two sentences that answer the question.
1. How many lenses are used in a compound microscope?
2. How do we figure how much a microscope magnifies?
3. What is the purpose of the adjustment knob on a microscope?
4. Why must an object be translucent in order for it to be viewed under a microscope?

## Word tools

Complete each statement by choosing a term from the list. (One term will not be used.)

1. The lens closest to the slide is the _____.
2. The adjustment knobs are used for _____.
3. The mirror _____.
4. The base _____.
5. The clips _____.
6. Objects which let some light through them are _____.

translucent
reflects light
holds the slide
supports the microscope
objective
focusing
eye lens

## Knowing what and why

A. *Number, Please . . .*
1. Suppose a microscope has an eye lens with a power of 10x and a low-power objective lens of 12x. How much does this microscope magnify under *low* power?
2. Suppose in the same microscope there is a high-power objective lens of 35x. How much does this microscope magnify under *high* power?

B. *Analyzing the Investigation*
Study Investigation 9. Answer the questions below.
1. Are the cells scraped off dead or alive? Explain.

2. Why do you see more cells under low power than under high power?
3. What is the job of the *cover glass*?
4. Suppose you used a blue stain instead of iodine. What would you see?

C. *On the Ladder of Understanding*
Use a dictionary to answer these questions.
1. In the word microscope, *micro* means _____.
2. In the word translucent, *trans* means _____.
3. In the word indigestion, *in* means _____.
4. In the word excretion, *ex* means _____.

## Looking further

1. You can buy a good hand lens rather cheaply. It will give you a great deal of pleasure to examine small objects with it. Examine the following: bread mold, insect, leaf, hair, or rocks.
2. Read about *lenses* in an encyclopedia. Write a report that answers these questions.

a. Which people are supposed to have invented lenses?
b. What materials are used to make lenses?
c. What do we call the process by which glass is made into a lens?
d. Name four occupations in which lenses may be useful.

What does the microscope show us about living things?

# The microscope and the unseen world

### 16-1. A new world comes into view

**TINY ANIMALS SEEN THROUGH MICROSCOPE**

___

**DUTCH SCIENTIST FINDS LIFE NEVER SEEN BEFORE**

___

Special to the Holland Express
DELFT, HOLLAND, January, 1675—Letters to the Royal Society of London.

**Fig. 106-1**

In 1492 Columbus entered a new world across the Atlantic. In 1969 Neil Armstrong walked on the moon. About midway between these years, a naturalist looked into a world of life as yet unseen.

The imaginary headline tells a story as it might have been told if it had happened today. Actually, this event occurred a long time ago. Read the headings and the Profile.

### 16-2. Nature's "Little League"

LEEUWENHOEK made careful notes and drew diagrams of the things he saw. He called the little animals "beasties." He wrote of his discovery to English and French scientists. They checked his work and found that it was true.

What had Leeuwenhoek actually found? He had discovered little animals that could carry on the same life activities as you do! Such simple animals are called PROTOZOA (proh-tuh-ZOH-uh), or "first animals." Later, other scientists found *plants* that were microscopic. Some examples of these tiny plants and animals may be seen on page 109.

## PROFILE OF A GREAT SCIENTIST     Anton van Leeuwenhoek

Anton van Leeuwenhoek (LAY-vun-hook), a Dutchman, worked as a janitor in the City Hall of Delft in Holland. He had an interesting hobby. He made lenses by carefully grinding glass.

With these lenses Leeuwenhoek examined everything he could find: drops of rainwater, tiny insects, saliva, decaying plants, yeast, and hundreds of other objects and materials. He only used these lenses singly—as a simple microscope. But they were very powerful lenses. They could magnify things many times their true size.

Leeuwenhoek is thought to have made 247 such microscopes. Some of these magnified objects 270 times their size! He observed bacteria, one-celled animals, human sperm, muscle and red blood cells.

He was honored for his work by being elected a member of the Royal Society of London, a society of the world's outstanding scientists.

Anton van Leeuwenhoek
1632–1723

## 16-3. The building blocks of living things

At the same time Leeuwenhoek was studying his "beasties" (1665), an English scientist named ROBERT HOOKE was studying the parts of plants. One day, looking through a compound microscope at a piece of cork, he noticed the cork had a regular pattern. Look at Figure 107-1.

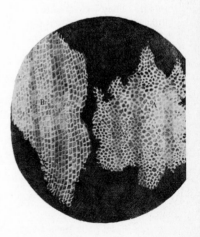

Fig. 107-1
Drawing of cork from Hooke's notebook.

> *I cut an exceeding thin piece of cork, placing it on a black object Plate. I could plainly perceive it to be all perforated and porous, much like a Honey-comb. These pores, or cells, were not very deep. These were the first <u>microscopical</u> pores I ever saw, and perhaps, that were ever seen, for I had not met with any Writer or Person that had made any mention of them before.*

To Hooke, the cork looked like it was made of many tiny "rooms" much like the honeycomb of a bee. He called them *cella,* the Latin word for room. In English we say CELL.

**Fig. 108-1**

Since the cork was part of a tree that was once alive, Hooke thought that *all* living things might be made of cells. With further study, he and other scientists continued to find that living things contained cells.

### 16-4. The cell theory

By 1838 most scientists were convinced that all living things were made of cells. The CELL THEORY was then announced. Today the cell theory is an accepted scientific idea.

Look at the pictures on page 109. Each of these microscopic creatures is made of *only one* cell. Other plants and animals, including human beings, contain millions or even billions of cells.

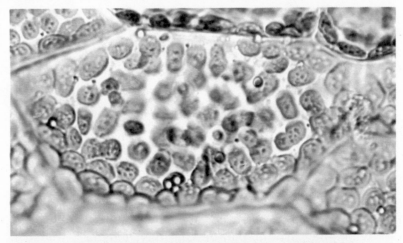

**Fig. 108-2**

Example of a plant cell. The green structures are *chloroplasts*. They help plants make food and contain *chlorophyll*.

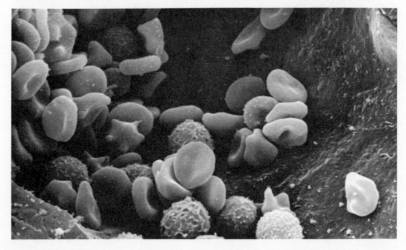

**Fig. 108-3**

Example of human cells. These blood cells have been magnified almost 3,000 times their real size. Why are cells often called the building blocks of life?

**PROTOZOA**
microscopic
animals

**PARAMECIUM** (PAR-uh-MEE-see-um)
Animal with unchanging shape. Swims
about by using hairs called CILIA (SIL-
ee-uh). Fig. 109-1

**Fig. 109-1**

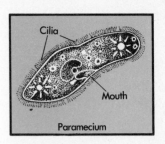

**AMEBA** (uh-MEE-buh)
Animal that keeps changing shape. Surrounds food to digest it. Fig. 109-2

**Fig. 109-2**

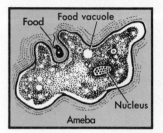

**FUNGI**
(FUN-jy)
plants
without
green-plant
color

**BACTERIA** (bak-TEER-ee-uh)
Simple colorless plants that cannot make
their own food. Some cause diseases. Some
are rod-shaped (a). Some are ball-shaped (b),
and some are shaped like corkscrews (c).
Fig. 109-3

**Fig. 109-3**

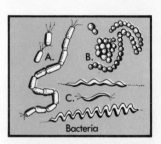

**YEAST** (YEEST)
Simple colorless plants. They reproduce by
growing buds which break off to form new
plants. Fig. 109-4

**Fig. 109-4**

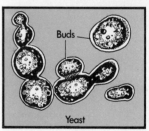

**ALGAE**
(AL-jee)
plants
containing
green-plant
color

**SPIROGYRA** (spy-roh-JY-ruh)
This green plant lives in ponds. The spiral-
shaped part contains CHLOROPHYLL
(KLOR-uh-fil), the green substance that
these plants use to make their own food.
Fig. 109-5

**Fig. 109-5**

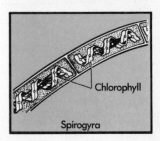

### 16-5. The grouping of living things

Most of us know of the groups called animals and those called plants. But under the microscope, some living things don't fit into either of these groups.

Some biologists place the protozoa and green algae into a separate group called PROTISTS (PROH-tists). Yeasts and other fungi are sometimes placed into a group all their own.

Usually, we talk of three groups of organisms: the animal kingdom, the plant kingdom, and the protist kingdom.

---

### Learned So Far . . .

- All living things are made of cells.
- Some simple plants and animals have only one cell.
- All life activities are carried out by one or more cells in the plant or animal.
- Organisms are usually grouped into three kingdoms: the plant, animal, and protist.

---

## SELF-STUDY GUIDE FOR CHAPTER 16

All answers should be written in your notebook. Please do not write in this book.

### *Understanding the reading*

A.  *Find the Answers*
    Write the letter of the correct answer.
    1. What is the main idea of Chapter 16?
        a. Leeuwenhoek is the "father" of microscopic study.
        b. Some living things are microscopic.
        c. Cells perform all life functions.
        d. Fungi are non-green plants.
    2. Leeuwenhoek used a simple microscope to discover
        a. the cell theory.
        b. microscopic life.
        c. cork cells.
        d. spirogyra.

    3. The cilia of a paramecium
        a. move it through the water.
        b. cause it to reproduce.
        c. do nothing.
        d. help digestion.
    4. Hooke saw and named cells in
        a. bacteria.
        b. ameba.
        c. yeast.
        d. cork.

B.  *True or False*
    If the statement is true, write *true*. If the

statement is false, change the word in *italics* to make the statement true.
1. Leeuwenhoek called his microscopic animals *critters*.
2. *Red blood cells* grow buds.
3. Both algae and corn plants get their color from *iron*.
4. *Beebe* named cells in living things.

C.  *Locate the Idea*
Find the sentence which answers each question. Write the sentence in your notebook.
1. Section 16-3: How were cells named?
2. Section 16-2: What are the "first animals"?

3. Figure 108-2: What do the chloroplasts contain?
4. Section 16-1: What are some things Leeuwenhoek studied?
5. Section 16-5: How are organisms grouped?

D.  *Find the "Outsider"*
Which word in each group of four does *not* belong with the others?
1. algae, spirogyra, chlorophyll, yeast
2. lens, slide, microscope, liter
3. geranium, bacteria, yeast, fungi
4. ameba, blood cell, paramecium, protozoa

## Knowing what and why

A.  *Understanding the Diagrams*
Look back to page 109. Answer the questions below.
1. What is the biggest difference between algae and fungi?
2. Give an example of an algae plant. What substance does it have to help make its food?
3. What is the difference between the way paramecium and ameba get their food? To what kingdom do they belong?

B.  *On the Ladder of Understanding*
Each word in the list is important to a living thing. Explain whether it concerns a plant and/or animal and with which life activity it is connected. Example: urea, in an animal, excretion. You may wish to review earlier chapters.
1. oxygen
2. photosynthesis
3. proteins
4. response

## Looking further

1. You can grow yeast cells. Follow these directions:
   a. Buy a small yeast cake in the supermarket.
   b. Put about 250 mL of water into a jar. Stir in 15 mL of sugar. Crumble half of the yeast cake into the sugar solution. Cover and let the jar stand at room temperature for two days.

   c. Bring the jar to class to have its contents examined under a microscope.

2. In an encyclopedia, read about *wine* or *beer* manufacture. Write a report for your class to show how yeast plants are used in manufacturing these beverages. What is the process called?

## chapter 17

TARGET    What can we see inside the cell?

# *A look inside the cell*

### 17-1. Putting the evidence together

Look at a brick wall from afar. It looks solid. Now come closer and look again. What do you see? You will probably notice that it is made of many bricks, each identical to one another. In the same way, all plants and animals are made of cells, the building blocks of all living things.

Many years have passed since the cell theory was announced in 1839. Since that time, many scientists have studied cells. Thousands of plants and animals have been *dissected*. As we learned earlier, to dissect is to cut up into smaller parts. These smaller parts could be examined with new and better microscopes that have been built. Also many chemical tests have been made on cells. When we put all the facts together, we can be sure of three things:

**1.** In general, most cells have the same appearance.
**2.** There are chemical actions taking place in all cells.
**3.** These chemical actions explain the life activities.

### 17-2. What does a cell look like?

Although there are many kinds of dogs, you can easily de-

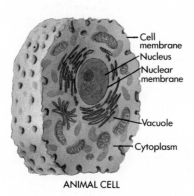

ANIMAL CELL

— Cell membrane
— Nucleus
— Nuclear membrane
— Vacuole
— Cytoplasm

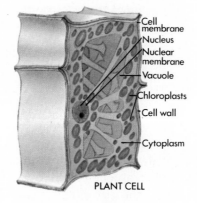

PLANT CELL

— Cell membrane
— Nucleus
— Nuclear membrane
— Vacuole
— Chloroplasts
— Cell wall
— Cytoplasm

**Fig. 113-1**

Compare these "typical" plant and animal cells. In what ways are they alike? In what ways are they different?

scribe in a *general* way what a dog—any dog—looks like. You can then go on to tell the difference between a shepherd and a collie. But, in general, all dogs have certain things in common. The same is true of cells. Plant cells differ somewhat from animal cells. In plants, there are many kinds of cells. In animals, also, there are many kinds of cells. But we can still describe a *typical* cell, a cell which in general is like all cells. The two diagrams in Fig. 113-1 show typical plant and animal cells.

### 17-3. Plant cell or animal cell?

The cells Hooke saw seemed to have a boundary or wall. We call this outside boundary of the cell the CELL WALL. Just inside the cell wall is another, thinner boundary called the CELL MEMBRANE. Compare the animal cell with the plant cell. *Both* cells have a cell membrane. But one chief difference between the two cells is that only the plant cell has a cell wall.

In Figure 109-4 a non-green plant cell is shown. Such cells are found in roots and stems. Other cells in leaves contain a green coloring. This green coloring comes from the chemical CHLOROPHYLL. Chlorophyll is contained in small, ball-shaped objects in the cell called CHLOROPLASTS (KLOR-uh-plasts). (Figure 108-2 in Chapter 16 shows plant cells of this type.)

Chlorophyll is not the only PIGMENT or material that gives a plant cell color. Many leaves also contain red and yellow pigments.

## Learned So Far . . .

- Plant cells differ from animal cells in that they have a cell wall outside of the cell membrane.
- Some plant cells have chloroplasts which contain chlorophyll. Such cells are green.
- Cells have length, width, and thickness.

### 17-4. Inside the cell

Just inside the cell membrane is a thick fluid very much like egg white. This is the CYTOPLASM (SY-tuh-plaz-um). Somewhere in the cytoplasm there appears a darker, ball-shaped object called the NUCLEUS (NEW-klee-us). Also inside the cytoplasm there are one or more "spaces" called VACUOLES (VAK-yoo-ohlz). Actually, these spaces are not empty. They are filled with water and dissolved chemicals. All these cell parts together make up what is known as *living matter*.

When Hooke first saw cork cells, he saw *only* the cell walls. The living matter had already died. By using fresh material, we can see the living matter of plants and animals.

## Do and Discover

Investigation 10: How can we show that green leaves contain chlorophyll?

### Procedures

1. Get a plant that has leaves which are both green and white—a silver-edged geranium for example. Heat several leaves (which have the two colors) in boiling water.
2. Transfer the leaves into hot alcohol, which has been placed in a water bath.
3. Remove the leaves and spread them on a glass plate.
   Warning: Do not boil alcohol near an open flame. Use an electric hot plate.

### Observations and Analysis

1. Why are the leaves boiled first?
2. Why are we using hot plates and not open-flame burners?
3. Does light pass through the chlorophyll mixture in the last picture?
4. What happened to the leaves?

Leaves in boiling water — Electric hotplate (1) Water bath (2) Leaves in hot alcohol — Glass plate (3) Chlorophyll in alcohol (4)

Fig. 114-1

## 17-5. Studying cells in the laboratory

Cutting and coloring are two special methods used to study cells. In order to examine cells with a microscope, a section of the plant or animal must be cut into thin slices. This allows light to pass through the cells, the microscope, and finally into our eyes.

When thin sections are prepared, the cells are often colorless. To see different parts of cells, dyes or stains are added to the cells. Not all the parts of the cells absorb the stain the same way. So the parts show up differently.

Sometimes scientists wish to separate parts of the cell from one another. By rapidly spinning test tubes full of cells, the heaviest parts settle to the bottom. The machine that does this is called a CENTRIFUGE (SEN-truh-fyooj). It is similar to the cream separator used to separate the parts of cow's milk. The spinning action forces the heavier parts of the milk to settle on the bottom. The cream remains at the top. If it is skimmed off the top, what is left is "skim" milk!

| SUMMARY OF CELL DATA | | |
|---|---|---|
| **Cell Shape** | can be | Spherical—like a marble<br>Rod—like a pencil<br>Rectangular—like a brick<br>Spiral—like a spring<br>Irregular—any shape |
| **Cell Size\*** | can be | Microscopic—1000 cells laid end to end will measure 1 cm.<br>Bird's eggs are exceptions. An ostrich egg, which is a single cell, is 20 cm in diameter |
| **Color** | can be | Colorless—like water or egg white<br>Green—if the cell has chlorophyll<br>Any color—depending on the color of the chemicals in the cytoplasm |
| **Physical State** | can be | Hard—as in bone or wood<br>Soft—as in skin or leaves |

Note:   Cell size is measured in MICRONS (MY-kronz) or *micrometers*. A micron is equal to one-millionth of a meter. The smallest object a naked human eye can see is 100 microns (1/100 of a cm).

## SELF-STUDY GUIDE FOR CHAPTER 17

All answers should be written in your notebook. Please do not write in this book.

### Understanding the reading

A.  *Find the Answers*
Write the letter of the correct answer.

1. Another title for Chapter 17 could be
   a. Not All Cells Are Alike.
   b. The Structure of Cells.
   c. Life Inside a Cell.
   d. Unknown Facts About Cells.
2. Living matter includes
   a. cytoplasm and a nucleus.
   b. a cell wall and a nucleus.
   c. a cell wall and a cell membrane.
   d. a vacuole and a cell wall.
3. A cell wall is found in the cells of
   a. bacteria only.
   b. all plants.
   c. only green plants.
   d. all living things.

4. The cells which Hooke first saw in cork consisted of
   a. a nucleus and cytoplasm.
   b. a nucleus and a vacuole.
   c. cell walls only.
   d. chloroplasts and a nucleus.

B.  *Locate the Idea*
Find the section in which each of these questions is answered. Write the number of the section and one or two sentences that answer the question.
1. What is a "typical" cell?
2. What is cytoplasm?
3. What is a chloroplast?
4. What does a vacuole look like?
5. What is the difference between a cell wall and a cell membrane?

### Word tools

Complete the paragraph by choosing the correct words from the list. No word may be used more than once. (Two words will not be used.)

Plant cells have a __(1)__ , but animal cells do not. All cells contain a thick fluid called __(2)__ . A darker, ball-shaped object in the cell is called the __(3)__ . Some cells are colorless. The color of those with chloroplasts is __(4)__ .

cell membrane
cell wall
green
nucleus
cytoplasm
vacuole

### Knowing what and why

A.  *Understanding the Diagram*
Look back to Figure 113-1. Examine the two cells.

1. Cover the labels with a sheet of paper. Now try to name the parts. Repeat this several times. You will soon learn the parts of the cells.
2. Now, still covering the labels, write the

names of each part into your notebook. Next to each part write its description.

B.  *What's the Difference?*
In a sentence or two, explain the difference between the words in each pair.
1. chloroplast–chlorophyll
2. cell wall–cell membrane
3. root cell–leaf cell

C.  *On the Ladder of Understanding*
Complete the statements. You may wish to review earlier chapters.

1.  A kilogram contains _____ grams.

2.  Nutrition robbers are called _____.
3.  Salts and _____ are dissolved in water to form urine.
4.  The naturalist's "field glasses" are also called _____.

D.  *Fun with Knowledge*
Copy the following puzzle and try to solve it.

Across
1.  Contains chlorophyll
4.  Single-celled plants
6.  A type of fungus
8.  A cell part found in plants only

Down
1.  Help paramecia move
2.  Protozoa are made of _____ _____ only
3.  Must live on or in another living thing
5.  _____ van Leeuwenhoek
6.  Short for mother
7.  Not young

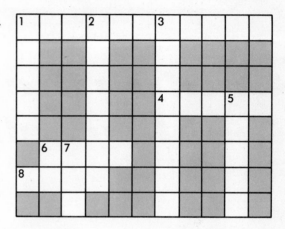

**Fig. 117-1**

*Looking further*

1.  Using modeling clay or balsa wood, make a model of a typical cell. Bring your work to class.
2.  Collect pictures of plants of different colors. Paste them on paper. Explain what gives these plants their colors.
(Hint: look for beets, carrots, turnips, green beans, or corn.)

## chapter 18

**TARGET** How does a cell do its work?

# *Getting the work done inside a cell*

### 18-1. Which part does what?

By this time you have probably guessed that each part of a cell has a different job. How can we find out what the job of each part is? There are two ways:

1. The shape, the form, and the location of the part will give us some clue about its job.

2. The study of its chemical make-up can tell us the job of each cell part.

### 18-2. The cell membrane for entrance and exit

You have already learned the word *absorb*. It means "to take in." You have also learned the word *excrete*. Do you remember that it means "to send out"?

Observe your teacher do this demonstration. It shows how membranes control what materials pass through it.

## Teacher Demonstration

Investigation 11: How do membranes control passing of materials through them?

### Procedures

1. Prepare the test tube with the phenolphthalein solution and cellophane membrane as shown.
2. Lower the test tube into the bottle of ammonia gas.

### Observations and Analysis

1. What color change do you see?
2. What is the action of the membrane?
3. Explain what you learned about the action of a cell membrane.

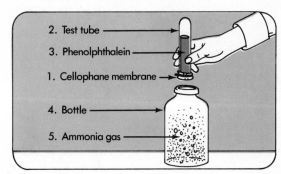

2. Test tube
3. Phenolphthalein
1. Cellophane membrane
4. Bottle
5. Ammonia gas

**Fig. 119-1**

## 18-3. Control by cell membranes

Look back to Chapter 12. You learned about absorption and excretion—taking in and giving out. In respiration, oxygen is absorbed and carbon dioxide and water are excreted. The processes of absorption and excretion are controlled by the cell membrane. All things going in or out of a cell must pass through the cell membrane. The cell membrane is *not* solid. It has very small holes, or *pores,* which control what passes in and out of the cell.

## Do and Discover

Investigation 12: Do dissolved materials pass through a cell membrane?

### Procedures

1. Prepare test tubes A and B as shown. Use any vegetable dye.
2. Lower test tube B into the beaker for an hour or two.

### Observations and Analysis

1. Record all color changes.
2. Explain the changes.
3. Why is test tube A called a *control?*
4. How does this investigation differ from Investigation 11?

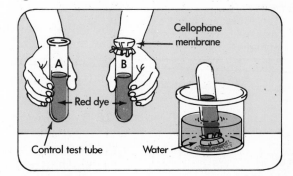

Cellophane membrane
A
B
Red dye
Control test tube
Water

**Fig. 119-2**

### 18-4. Cell walls for support and strength

Early scientists noticed that plant cells were generally more definite in their shape than animal cells. They soon realized that it was the thick cell walls that gave the plant cells support. Chemical tests showed that cell walls contain a compound called CELLULOSE (SEL-yuh-lohs). Cellulose is *not* alive. As the cell grows, it makes the compound cellulose from food and stores it around the cell membrane. Now we can explain why trees are hard and strong. Trees have wood cells which have very thick cell walls made of cellulose. When the trees die, the cell walls remain. We can cut the trees into lumber. Cotton fibers around cotton seeds also contain a great deal of cellulose. This is why cotton thread is strong. There is also a plant called flax which has strong cellulose fibers. These fibers are used to make linen cloth.

### Learned So Far . . .

- All cell membranes are alive. They control absorption and excretion.
- Cell walls, found only in plants, contain a nonliving material called cellulose.
- Cell walls give strength and support to plant cells.

### 18-5. The nucleus for growth and control

The human red blood cell loses its nucleus when it matures.

Scientists use tiny, delicate needles to dissect parts of a cell under a microscope. Slowly and very carefully, scientists can remove the nucleus. Even without a nucleus the cell continues to work for a short time. But soon the cell is no longer able to grow. It cannot reproduce. Chemical tests show that the nucleus is made of very complicated proteins. These proteins control assimilation (change of food into living matter), growth, and reproduction.

### 18-6. Living matter

Perhaps you have read about alchemists. They were men who spent their entire lives trying to find some magic way to change cheap metals into gold. They never succeeded. An even deeper secret is the ability of all organisms to make living matter. Although we can now tell what chemicals are found in living matter, we cannot put these chemicals together to make this "magic life stuff." This means that all living matter now in existence has come from other living matter. This colorless liquid is sometimes thin like water, sometimes thick like molasses. It is a mixture of ordinary elements and compounds. But it is the mixture that is the substance of life.

We use the term *living matter* to describe the substance found in living cells. Early biologists used the term PROTOPLASM.

## 18-7. The chemistry of living matter

Figure 121-1 shows the approximate amounts of elements and compounds which make up living matter. Think about these two important facts. First, living matter is a mixture of elements and compounds. Second, there are chemical actions going on in cells all the time. That is why the composition of living matter keeps changing. For example, after digestion a cell may have more sugar. As respiration takes place, it may have more carbon dioxide and less oxygen.

The chemistry of cells is controlled by substances called NUCLEIC (new-KLEE-ik) ACIDS. The most important of these acids are DNA and RNA. DNA is found only in the nucleus. It "programs" the "blueprint" which makes offspring look like their parents. In other words, it controls HEREDITY (huh-RED-ih-tee).

DNA is short for a very long chemical name—*deoxyribonucleic acid*. Try to pronounce it!

**THE CHEMICAL MAKE-UP OF LIVING MATTER**

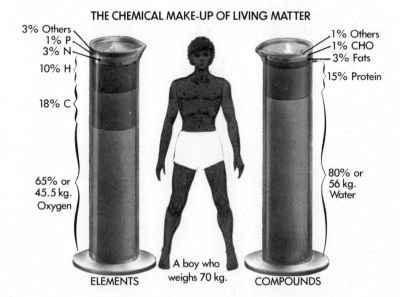

3% Others
1% P
3% N
10% H
18% C
65% or 45.5 kg. Oxygen

ELEMENTS

A boy who weighs 70 kg.

1% Others
1% CHO
3% Fats
15% Protein
80% or 56 kg. Water

COMPOUNDS

**Fig. 121-1**

Living matter contains ordinary elements and compounds in the approximate amounts shown above. This boy weighs 70 kg. If he weighed 90 kg, how many kilograms of water would there be in the boy's body?

### Learned So Far . . .

● Living matter is a complicated mixture of elements and compounds.
● As the life processes go on in cells, the composition of living matter changes.
● All life activities take place in living matter.

## Do and Discover

Investigation 13: Can salt, dissolved in water, pass through a cell membrane?

### Procedures

1. Dissolve one teaspoonful of table salt in a jar of water. Place salty water (A) in a clean medicine bottle (B). Cover with cellophane (C) and secure with a rubber band. Turn the medicine bottle upside down in a jar (D) half filled with clear tap water (E).
2. Allow to stand for 24 hours. Dip a wood splint into the jar. Taste the splint.

### Observations and Analysis

1. What taste do you get from the splint? What does this show?
2. What life activities are controlled by this process?

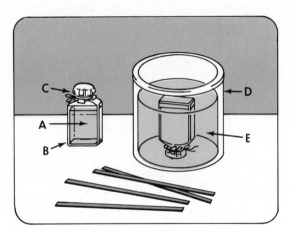

**Fig. 122-1**

## SELF-STUDY GUIDE FOR CHAPTER 18

All answers should be written in your notebook. Please do not write in this book.

*Understanding the reading* ⎯⎯⎯⎯⎯⎯⎯⎯⎯⎯⎯⎯⎯⎯⎯⎯

A. *Find the Answers*
  Write the letter of the correct answer.
  1. What is the main idea of Chapter 18?

  a. Living material is made of elements and compounds.

b. The parts of a cell have different jobs to do.

c. The cell wall is very different from the cell membrane.

d. The nucleus controls cell growth.

2. Wood gets its strength from
   a. its bark.
   b. the water it stores.
   c. the cellulose in its cell walls.
   d. DNA.

3. Cells are able to absorb
   a. liquids only.
   b. liquids and gases.
   c. gases only.
   d. elements only.

4. The amount of sugar in a cell
   a. is always the same.

b. is always changing.

c. is not known to scientists.

d. determines whether it is a plant or animal cell.

B. *Locate the Idea*
Find the sentence which answers each question. Write the sentence in your notebook.

1. Section 18-4: How is cellulose made?
2. Section 18-7: What chemicals control heredity?
3. Section 18-2: What part of a cell controls excretion?
4. Section 18-5: What two activities cannot go on when a cell nucleus is removed?
5. Section 18-7: Where is DNA found?

## Knowing what and why

A. *Explanation, Please . . .*
Answer in one or two sentences.

1. What part of a cell controls absorption?
2. Is living matter an element, a compound, or a mixture?
3. Why do the contents of living matter keep changing?
4. Which parts of a cell are *not* alive?

B. *Understanding the Chart*
Look back to Figure 121-1, the *Chemical Make-up of Living Matter.* Answer the questions below.

1. Hydrogen is shown as 10% of the elements. In which *compounds* at the right is the H present?

2. In which compound is most of the N found?
3. What is your mass in kilograms? How many kg of water do you contain? How many kg of oxygen do you contain?

C. *Number, Please . . .*
Supply the correct word or number. Write them in your notebook.
In living matter:

1. The most plentiful compound is _____, in the amount of _____ percent.
2. The most plentiful element is _____, in the amount of _____ percent.
3. The amount of nitrogen is _____ percent.
4. The amount of carbon is _____ percent.

## Looking further

1. In an encyclopedia, look up *cotton, flax,* and *hemp.* Relate your reading to cellulose. Give a brief description of how the fibers are used to make cotton, rope, and linen.

2. From your local Heart Association, obtain literature which explains the relationship between salt (sodium chloride) and high blood pressure. Write a report.

**TARGET**  How do groups of cells work together to perform life functions?

# Teamwork among cells

### 19-1. All the work or a special job?

In an automobile plant, no one person puts the whole car together. There are "body workers" who attach fenders and doors. There are "spring workers" who put the springs in place. There are "engine workers" who install the engine, and so forth. The specialists add up to teamwork. In this chapter, we will look at the teamwork inside of living things.

In Chapter 16 of this unit, we saw that some plants, such as bacteria and yeasts, and some animals, such as amebas and paramecia, consist of only *one* cell. Of course, all life activities in each of these cases must be done by that one cell. But what happens in *many-celled* plants and animals?

### 19-2. Cells as teams

The microscope helps us see the wonderful story of teamwork. We see that animals and plants are not just big masses of cells. We see that there are different *kinds* of cells and that cells form *groups*. The cells in these groups resemble each other in appearance. Of course, each cell must carry on *all* life activities. But because of their different structure, some cells are able to do one life task better than any other. When a cell concentrates on one life task we say that it is SPE-CIALIZED (SPESH-uh-lyzd). Groups of cells that look alike and work together in a special life activity are called TISSUES (TISH-ooz).

## 19-3. Covering tissues

Which of the tissues in your body is most visible to you? The tissue of your skin of course. And what do you think is its special job? It covers the cells below the surface. If you have ever fallen and scraped the top layer of skin, you were able to see the "raw" layers below. This is a clue to another job of covering tissue—it protects. The scientist's name for skin cells is EPITHELIAL (ep-uh-THEE-lee-ul) tissue.

Epithelial tissue is found largely in the skin and in the linings of the body, where it covers the organs inside your body.

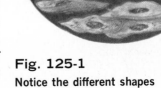

**Fig. 125-1**
Notice the different shapes of cells which make up epithelial tissue.

## Learned So Far . . .

- Like cells work together as tissues.
- Epithelial tissue is one kind of tissue.
- Epithelial tissue covers and protects.

## 19-4. Tissues for support

Most "higher" animals have a frame, or SKELETON, to support the body. The skeleton consists of hard bone tissue.

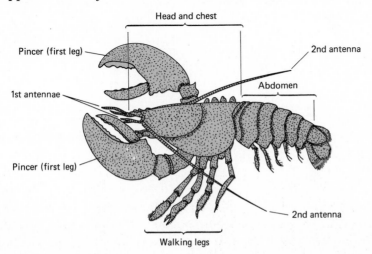

Head and chest

Pincer (first leg)

2nd antenna

1st antennae

Abdomen

Pincer (first leg)

2nd antenna

Walking legs

**Fig. 125-2**
The lobster has a skeleton on the outside! Explain the teamwork in this skeleton.

Under the microscope, it can be observed that living bone cells contain soft cytoplasm. However, between the cells there are deposits of nonliving, hard compounds of *calcium* and *phosphorus*. It takes a hard blow to break a bone. Bones are even strong enough to support the weight of an elephant!

Can you bend your ear? Can you bend the tip of your nose? Yes, but when you let go, the ear and nose spring back into place. The inner tissue of your ear is a flexible supporting tissue called CARTILAGE (KAR-tuh-lij). Cartilage is also found in the joints of bones, where it works as a shock absorber. For example, the knee joint has cartilage pads. When you jump, the shock is absorbed in your knees so that you feel the shock less in your spine, shoulders, and head.

## Do and Discover

Investigation 14: What minerals give strength to bones?

**Procedures**
1. Leave a bone in a jar of vinegar for a few days.
2. Wash the bone. Try to bend it.

**Observations and Analysis**
1. How has the bone changed?
2. What does the vinegar (acetic acid) do to the calcium?
3. Can you name some other acids?

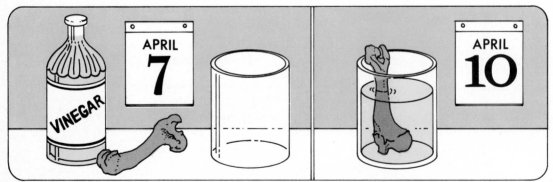

Fig. 126-1

### 19-5. Tissues to move and work

Muscle tissue is made of cells which have no cell membranes between them and, therefore, appear as "bands" or "stripes." These bands grow longer or shorter to lengthen or shorten

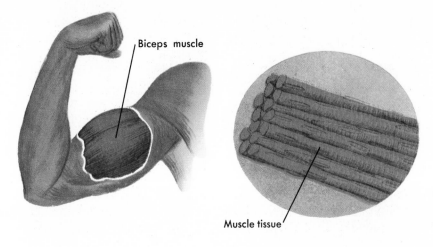

Biceps muscle

Muscle tissue

Fig. 127-1
Muscle tissue is used for locomotion and work.

the muscle. Can you "make a muscle" in your arm? This muscle is called the BICEPS (BY-seps). Notice how you bend the arm at the elbow to make the biceps hard. You can choose to do this or choose not to do it. This muscle, like most muscles in your body, is controlled by your will. It is called a VOLUNTARY MUSCLE. There are some muscles in your body that are INVOLUNTARY—*not* under the control of your will. The muscles in the walls of your heart and in the walls of your stomach are examples of involuntary muscles.

Most muscles work in pairs. Can you name several pairs of muscles?

### 19-6. Tissues to connect

Would you believe it? There are 206 bones in the human skeleton. How do they "hang together"? There is a strong connecting tissue which forms LIGAMENTS (LIG-uh-munts) that hold the bones together. There is also a connecting tissue which attaches bones to muscles so that the muscles have a firm hold for moving the bones. This connecting tissue is formed from cells that have fibers in them. Fibers which connect muscles to bones are called TENDONS (TEN-dunz). Strain or poor use of your body may cause you to stretch a ligament or a tendon. You will then have much pain and may be unable to move your arm or leg or shoulder. Doctors suggest rest, hot baths, and massage to help the ligaments and tendons to heal.

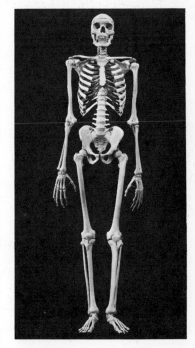

Fig. 127-2
The human skeleton is very similar to most vertebrate skeletons. In what ways could the human skeleton be called a machine?

127

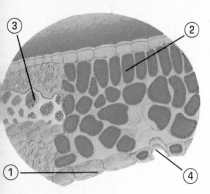

**Fig. 128-1**

A microscopic view through a typical leaf. What is the function of each part?

## 19-7. The tissues of plants

So far we have mentioned tissues, organs, and systems in *animals*. There are also *plant* tissues. Look at the diagram in Figure 128-1. Notice that the cells on the outside of the leaf (1) are all similar. You can guess that these cells, which are called the EPIDERMIS (ep-ih-DER-mis), are like epithelial tissue. The epidermis covers the top and bottom of the leaf and protects the inside cells. Now notice that the inside cells (2) are green. They contain chloroplasts and chlorophyll. As you learned before, this tissue can make food for the plant. The SPONGY CELLS (3) form a tissue with large spaces to store oxygen and carbon dioxide. These gases move in and out of leaves through the openings called STOMATES (STOH-mayts) (4).

Stems and roots in plants have special tissues to carry water and dissolved foods. Tree trunks have growing tissue called CAMBIUM (KAM-bee-um). Cambium grows to form woody tissue and long water-carrying tubes.

### Learned So Far . . .

- In animals, bone and cartilage tissue give strength and support.
- Muscle tissue is used for locomotion and work.
- Ligaments and tendons hold bones and muscles together.
- Plants have specialized tissues for special jobs.

## SELF-STUDY GUIDE FOR CHAPTER 19

All answers should be written in your notebook. Please do not write in this book.

*Understanding the reading*

A. *Find the Answers*
   Write the letter of the correct answer.
   1. Another title for Chapter 19 could be
      a. Many Kinds of Cells.
      b. Muscle and Bones.
      c. Tendons, Ligaments, Muscles, and Bones.
      d. Cells Form Tissues.

   2. In Section 19-7, the reading teaches us that
      a. plants are more specialized than animals.
      b. the epidermis is like epithelial tissue.
      c. plants are not specialized at all.
      d. there is only one plant tissue—cambium.

3. Tissues are formed from groups of
   a. similar cells doing the same jobs.
   b. similar cells doing different jobs.
   c. different cells doing different jobs.
   d. different cells doing the same job.
4. Tendons are *most* like
   a. cartilage cells.
   b. voluntary muscles.
   c. biceps.
   d. ligaments.

B. *Locate the Idea*
Find the section in which each of these questions is answered. Write the number of the section and one or two sentences that answer the question.
1. What is the scientist's name for skin cells?
2. What is the difference between a tendon and a ligament?
3. Why is bone hard?
4. What is the meaning of "tissue"?

## Word tools

Find the correct definition from *Column B* which describes the word in *Column A*. (One definition will not be used.)

**Column A**
1. specialized cells
2. bones
3. tendons
4. involuntary muscle
5. biceps

**Column B**
a. connects muscles to bones
b. tissues
c. arm muscle
d. connects bones together
e. stomach wall
f. phosphorus found in these

## Knowing what and why

A. *True or False?*
Write if the statement is true or false. Then explain your answer in one or two sentences.
1. Milk can be a "bone builder."
2. All skin tissue is alive.
3. Most house plants have very little cambium tissue.
4. Ligaments hold muscles together.

B. *What's the Difference?*
In a sentence or two, explain the difference between the two words in each pair.
1. ligaments–tendons
2. epidermis–epithelial
3. biceps–triceps
4. chloroplast–chlorophyll

C. *On the Ladder of Understanding*
Complete the statements. You may wish to review earlier chapters.

1. Phosphorus and calcium are (elements, compounds).
2. The nucleus of a muscle cell controls (growth, absorption).
3. The outer boundary of a cartilage cell is the (cell wall, cell membrane).
4. The skin can receive a (stimulus, response).

D. *Puzzling It Out*
Answer these questions in a sentence or two.
1. Why will smearing petroleum jelly on the bottom surface of a green plant's leaves kill the plant?
2. Name three tissues found in your windpipe. What does each one do to make the windpipe work properly?

## chapter 20

**TARGET**  Which tissues command and control other tissues?

# *Tissues in command and control*

Fig. 130-1

### 20-1. Blood, the life-giving fluid

A siren screams in the middle of the night. An ambulance races to deliver a bottle of precious liquid. It is PLASMA (PLAZ-muh)—the life-giving fluid in blood. Somewhere down the road, there has been an accident. The victim is in shock. He lies pale and weak from loss of blood. Soon the ambulance arrives, and the ambulance doctor gives the man a TRANS-FUSION (trans-FYOO-zhun). After a short time, his color begins to return and he breathes more easily.

### 20-2. What is blood? What are its functions?

In the body of an average person weighing 65 kg, there are about 5 L (or 5000 mL) of a red liquid called blood. Blood is a tissue because it is made up of cells. Blood is different from other tissues, of course, because most of it is a liquid.

If you examine a drop of blood under the microscope, you would find that blood is made of many parts. So you can guess that blood has many functions. Overall, however, we can say that blood is a TRANSPORT tissue. It carries materials around the body of the animal. As the blood moves around the body we say it CIRCULATES (SUR-kyuh-layts).

## Learned So Far . . .

- Blood is a liquid tissue with cells floating in it.
- Blood is a transport tissue. It circulates all through the body.

### 20-3. The liquid part of the blood

The liquid part of the blood is called plasma. It is a pale yellow liquid, mostly water. Look at Fig. 131-1. Plasma is 92% water. The rest of the plasma contains other chemicals.

The amount of each of these other chemicals is always changing. A few hours after a good meal, there may be a great deal of sugar in your plasma. After vigorous exercise in the gym, your plasma contains a great deal of carbon dioxide. On a hot summer day, after you have perspired, there will be less salt in your plasma than on cooler days.

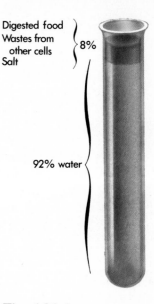

Digested food
Wastes from
other cells
Salt
} 8%

92% water

**Fig. 131-1**
**The composition of plasma.**

## Learned So Far . . .

- Plasma is the liquid part of the blood.
- Plasma contains cells and dissolved chemicals.

### 20-4. Blood cells

A drop of blood under the microscope shows three kinds of cells. You can easily see two kinds of cells. The third is harder to see. First, there are about five million RED BLOOD CELLS. These cells have no nuclei. Chemical tests show that they get their red color from a compound of iron called

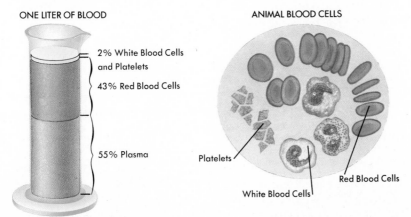

ONE LITER OF BLOOD

2% White Blood Cells and Platelets

43% Red Blood Cells

55% Plasma

ANIMAL BLOOD CELLS

Platelets

White Blood Cells

Red Blood Cells

**Fig. 131-2**
**The composition of blood.**

HEMOGLOBIN (HEE-muh-gloh-bin). Second, there are about eight thousand WHITE BLOOD CELLS. These look like the ameba you studied earlier. Third, there are small, irregular cells called PLATELETS (PLAYT-lets).

### 20-5. What is the work of red blood cells?

| RED BLOOD CELLS | In the Lungs: hemoglobin combines with oxygen. |
| | At the Cells: oxyhemoglobin gives off oxygen. |

Hemoglobin can form a temporary compound with oxygen. This temporary compound is called OXYHEMOGLOBIN. Oxygen joins with hemoglobin in the lungs, where air is breathed in. Blood carries the oxyhemoglobin to all cells. There the oxygen is absorbed by the cells. The red blood cells are now left with hemoglobin.

### 20-6. What is the work of the other blood cells?

When you are healthy, a drop of your blood may contain about eight thousand white blood cells. When certain germs make you sick, however, there is a sudden increase in the number of white blood cells. Your "blood count" goes up. What happens is similar to a country drafting soldiers in time of war. When "enemy" germs invade our blood, our white blood cells go off to battle them. They surround and "swallow" the invaders. Sometimes white blood cells lose the battle, though. The germs detroy them and the result is PUS, the dead white blood cells and dead germs.

The platelets are much smaller than red blood cells and have irregular shapes. The platelets give off a chemical that causes the blood to clot at certain times. For example, when you cut yourself the blood clots at the wound to cut off the flow of any more blood. This saves you from losing a great deal of blood.

### Learned So Far . . .

- White blood cells destroy germs.
- Platelets begin clotting.

### 20-7. Blood controls many life functions

Why does the title of this chapter suggest that blood "commands" and "controls" other tissues? Let us remember what we read before. Blood carries digested food to all cells. Blood carries oxygen to all the cells. This oxygen produces energy through the oxidation of food. Blood fights disease all over the body. No wonder blood has been called the "life-giving" liquid!

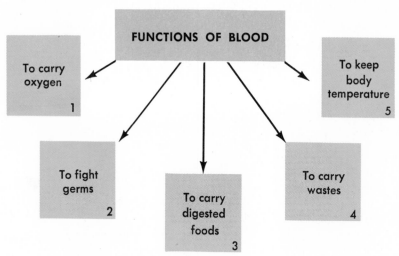

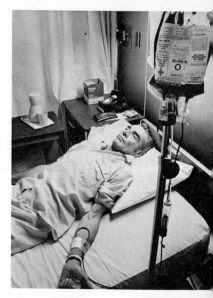

**Fig. 133-1**

A blood transfusion can save a life.

## 20-8. When you lose blood

When a patient has lost a lot of blood, new blood can be put into his or her body. The transfer of blood is called a *transfusion*. A transfusion can be made directly through a tube from one person to another. More often, the patient receives plasma or whole blood (plasma plus cells) from a laboratory which is called a BLOOD BANK. Blood banks store large amounts of blood for emergencies.

Human blood is found in four types: A, B, AB, and O.

## 20-9. Nerve tissue for communication and control

Earlier, we spoke of stimulus and response. We gave the example of your finger touching a hot stove and pulling away very quickly. To pull your arm away, muscles had to be "told" to pull the arm bones. In other words, a message had to be sent, a command had to be given, and an "order" had to be carried out. How was this done? When your finger touched the hot stove, nerve cells in the tip of your finger received a stimulus. The nerve cells instantly sent a message to your brain. The brain then "read" the message and decided that the stove was too hot to touch. A command was then sent

Some nerve cells grow to be two meters long. How does this compare to your height?

| ANIMAL SENSES | |
| --- | --- |
| **Sense** | **Organ** |
| Sight | Eyes |
| Smell | Nose |
| Hearing | Ears |
| Taste | Tongue |
| Touch | Skin |

from your brain to the muscles in your arm. The brain "ordered" the muscles to pull back your arm and your arm responded. All this took place in an instant, too quickly for you to know what was happening. Your body contains many nerve cells which make it possible for you to feel, see, hear, taste, and smell the world around you.

## Learned So Far . . .

- Senses pick up stimuli.
- Your nerve cells send messages to the brain, muscles, bones, and glands.

## SELF-STUDY GUIDE FOR CHAPTER 20

All answers should be written in your notebook. Please do not write in this book.

*Understanding the reading* _____

A. *Find the Answers*
Write the letter of the correct answer.
1. The number of white blood cells is greater when your tonsils are infected because white blood cells
   a. provide oxygen to give you energy.
   b. are needed to destroy germs.
   c. are found mostly in the region of the throat.
   d. stop shock.
2. Plasma is carried by army medics in powdered form because
   a. it is lighter.
   b. it is cheaper.
   c. it can give more energy.
   d. it can be taken by mouth.
3. People who have lost a great deal of blood are fed foods rich in iron because
   a. iron is needed to increase plasma.
   b. iron helps clotting.
   c. iron gives energy.
   d. iron is needed to form hemoglobin.

B. *True or False*
If the statement is true, write *true.* If the statement is false, change the word in *italics* to make it true.
1. Sugar is found in *plasma.*
2. White blood cells "swallow" *germs.*
3. *Capillaries* control clotting.
4. Nerve cells control *behavior.*

C. *Locate the Idea*
Find the section in which each of these questions is answered. Write the number of the section and one or two sentences that answer the question.
1. How is blood involved in producing energy?
2. What is "counted" in a blood count?
3. Where are large amounts of blood stored?
4. What type of tissue gives your arm muscle an "order" to pull away from a hot stove?

*Knowing what and why*

A. *Explanation, Please. . .*
Answer in one or two sentences.
1. What senses are for protection?
2. How can we treat shock?
3. How is a clot formed?
4. How is pus formed?

B. *Which Part? What Number?*
Answer the following questions in your notebook.
1. Which blood cells are the most numerous?
2. Which blood cells are the largest?
3. Which blood cell has the largest nucleus?
4. What forms more than half of blood?
5. What forms more than 90% of plasma?

6. How many liters of blood does an average person have?
7. "Eight thousand cells per drop" probably refers to which blood cells?
8. Which are the *longest* cells in the body?

C. *On the Ladder of Understanding*
Complete the statements.
1. Two elements found in hemoglobin are _____ and _____.
2. To see tissue under a microscope it must be _____.
3. The outer boundary of the white blood cell is called _____.
4. 92% of plasma has the formula _____.
5. The person who named cells was _____.

*Looking further*

Interview an official from your local hospital on the subject of blood banks. Use these questions to ask. Then write a report.
a. What is a blood bank?

b. What does it store?
c. How is it used?
d. How does someone join the local blood bank?

## chapter 21

**TARGET**  How do tissues combine to form the total plant or animal?

# *Teamwork among tissues*

### 21-1. Where are tissues found?

To answer this question, let us pick one small part of your body—your finger. The first thing you will probably notice is that your finger has a covering tissue. You already know that your finger has epithelial tissue. Now feel your finger for the bones. There are several bones and they are connected to each other. So your finger must have bone tissue and connective tissue. Can you move your finger? It is the muscle tissue which moves it. When you cut your finger, you feel pain with your nerve tissue. And the blood, flowing out of your cut, leaves no doubt that your finger contains blood tissue. And so the answer to the question above is this. Almost every part of your body has a little of each of the tissues.

### 21-2. Tissues into organs

Name a few parts of your body that do special jobs. The chances are that the part you name is an ORGAN. Here are examples of organs:

**heart—brain—lung—stomach—eye—kidney—skin**

Each of these parts is made up of at least one tissue and

usually more than one. For example, since the heart pumps the blood, it is mostly muscle tissue. But it also has connective fibers in its valves and epithelial tissue to cover it. The brain is your thinking and control organ. So it is mostly nerve tissue. But it also has blood in it.

## Learned So Far . . .

- An organ is one part of the body that has a special job.
- An organ has one or more tissues in it.

### 21-3. Organs into systems

Look back to Fig. 77-1 which shows you the parts of the body dealing with digestion. How many organs can you find? There is the mouth, liver, pancreas (PAN-kree-us), stomach, large intestine, and small intestine. In Section 2 we saw that each organ does a special job. Now we see a new team. Several organs that work together form a SYSTEM (SIS-tum). In this case, we are talking about the DIGESTIVE SYSTEM. Study the diagrams below for examples of other systems.

**RESPIRATORY SYSTEM**

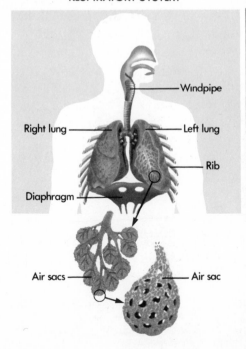

**CIRCULATORY SYSTEM**

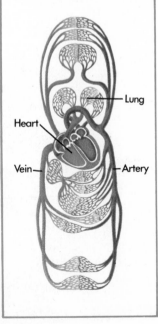

**Fig. 137-1**

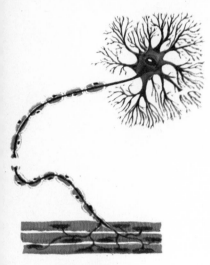

## 21-4. The nervous system

All of your nerve cells are in some way connected to your brain. This system of nerves is called the NERVOUS SYSTEM. The function of the nervous system is to carry stimuli to the brain so that the body can respond to the outside world. The nerve cell shown in Fig. 138-1 has long branches which connect with thousands of other nerve cells. These cells are called NEURONS (NEW-ronz). They are extremely sensitive. Sometimes, we respond without realizing what we are doing. For example, your arm pulls away from a hot object without your thought. This is called an INVOLUNTARY RESPONSE. Before a baseball player at bat swings at the pitched ball, he also uses nerve cells. However, his response is under the control of his brain and will. He may decide to swing or let the ball pass. This is called a VOLUNTARY RESPONSE.

**Fig. 138-1**

Why have these tissues been likened to a telephone system?

## 21-5. Plant organs

The major organs in most plants that you know are the roots, stems, and leaves. Some plants also have fruits and flowers. As in animals, several organs work together to form systems. In plants, the most important systems are the food-making system, the water-carrying system, and the reproduction system. Study Figure 138-2.

**Fig. 138-2**

The major parts of a typical plant.

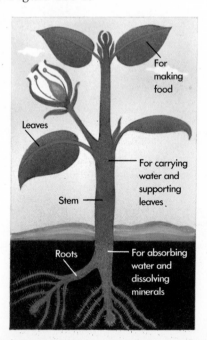

For making food

Leaves

For carrying water and supporting leaves

Stem

Roots

For absorbing water and dissolving minerals

# THE ARRANGEMENT OF LIVING PARTS

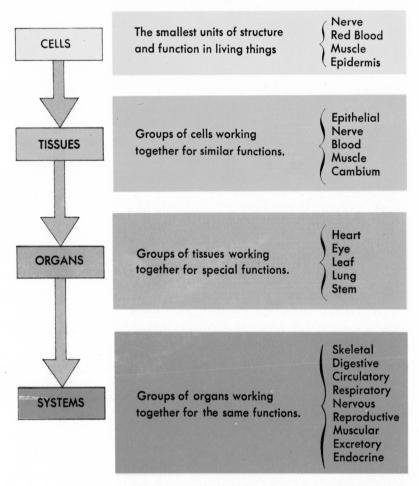

Living matter which makes up all living things.

| CELLS | The smallest units of structure and function in living things | Nerve<br>Red Blood<br>Muscle<br>Epidermis |

| TISSUES | Groups of cells working together for similar functions. | Epithelial<br>Nerve<br>Blood<br>Muscle<br>Cambium |

| ORGANS | Groups of tissues working together for special functions. | Heart<br>Eye<br>Leaf<br>Lung<br>Stem |

| SYSTEMS | Groups of organs working together for the same functions. | Skeletal<br>Digestive<br>Circulatory<br>Respiratory<br>Nervous<br>Reproductive<br>Muscular<br>Excretory<br>Endocrine |

Fig. 139-1

## SELF-STUDY GUIDE FOR CHAPTER 21

All answers should be written in your notebook. Please do not write in this book.

*Understanding the reading*

A. *Find the Answers*
   Write the letter of the correct answer.
   1. Another title for Chapter 21 could be
      a. Tissues Everywhere.
      b. All Parts Are Independent.
      c. Cells—Into Tissues—Into Organs.
      d. Cells: Different, Yet Alike.
   2. The digestive system contains the following organs:
      a. lungs, stomach, and mouth

b. windpipe, esophagus, and stomach
c. liver, small intestine, and windpipe
d. large intestine, small intestine, and esophagus

3. The brain is mostly
   a. bone tissue.
   b. connecting tissue.

c. nerve tissue.
d. all tissues.

4. Which of the following words is applied mostly to a *system?*
   a. cardiac
   b. circulatory
   c. gastric
   d. salivary

## Word tools

Complete the paragraph by choosing the correct words from the list. No word may be used more than once. (Two words will not be used.)

Cells which are alike and do a similar job are called __(1)__. Tissues are grouped together into specific parts of the body that we call __(2)__. A __(3)__ is made up of several organs that work together. An example of a cell is a __(4)__. An example of an organ is the __(5)__. An example of a system is the __(6)__ system.

neuron
system
respiratory
response
tissues
liver
organs
calcium

## Knowing what and why

A. *Explanation, Please . . .*
   Answer in one or two sentences.
   1. Does an organ contain more than one tissue? Explain.
   2. Why does Chapter 21 *not* apply to bacteria, ameba, and yeast?
   3. Are all our responses *voluntary?*

B. *On the Ladder of Understanding*
   Complete the statements. You may wish to review earlier chapters.
   1. The word *biome* is used in the study of (ecology, bacteriology).
   2. A scientific idea is "stronger" when it is (a hypothesis, a theory).

3. Blood volume is measured in (grams, liters).
4. A tapeworm has a well-organized (tissue, digestive system).

C. *Puzzling It Out*
   Look back to Figures 128-1 and 138-2. Answer these questions in a sentence or two.
   1. What part of a plant makes food?
   2. What are the parts of a typical leaf?
   3. How do gases go into and out of leaves?
   4. What is the layer of cells on the outside of the leaf?

## Looking further

1. Ask your English teacher to help you find a copy of the poem "Trees" by Joyce Kilmer. You will enjoy reading it.

2. Make your own color chart of the respiratory, circulatory, or digestive system. Bring it in for your class.

# UNIT V

# *The behavior of living things*

## Unit V / outline

# The behavior of living things

## What's it all about?

Have you heard the saying, "The left hand doesn't know what the right hand is doing"? This means that each hand works independently of the other. Many times the hands work together. They are COORDINATED (koh-OR-duh-nayt-ed). When a football player reaches up to catch a pass, both hands grasp the ball. The hands are coordinated. But if one hand closes and the other hand does not, the hands are not working together. The player will probably drop the ball.

We know that our hands must be coordinated for certain work. But what about the other parts of the body? Imagine if they all worked separately, without control! How would your throat know when to swallow? When would your eyes blink? How would we walk up a flight of stairs? How would a horse run in a field?

These are all questions about BEHAVIOR and RESPONSE.

The kind of behavior we spoke of above is generally a response to the environment. But there are also responses that control the "inner" workings of the body.

In this unit, you will
* study the control of behavior.
* see how specialized tissues and organs receive sensations and carry out responses.
* see how special chemicals affect behavior.

*And just as important,* you will
* learn about learning itself.
* get an idea of how human behavior is shaped.

## chapter 22

**TARGET**   How do living things respond to their environment?

# *Responses help living things function*

## 22-1. Looking back . . .

Turn back to Chapter 9. Re-read Sections 9-1 through 9-5. In summary, you have now reviewed the major ideas about living responses. There are changes in the environment. These changes act as stimuli. The plant or animal responds to the stimuli.

## 22-2. The meaning of behavior

**Fig. 144-1**

How is this web a response to environment?

A cockroach runs away from a bright light. Protozoa swim away from electricity or acid. Dust in the nose makes an animal sneeze. A beaver spends months building its home. The spider carefully spins a web. A plant bends toward the light. When the temperature drops, some birds go to a warmer climate. When you see a green traffic light, you know it is safe to cross the street. You "remember" the day and date. You speak words, sing a song, whistle a tune, and type a letter. These are all examples of the activities of living things. This is *behavior*.

When we use the word *behavior* in biology, we mean *all of the responses of an organism*. Behavior means one or more responses to one or more stimuli. Behavior is, therefore, a response to the environment. It shows us how an organism has adapted to its environment.

## Learned So Far . . .

- A stimulus is a change in the surroundings of a plant or animal that causes a response.
- Responses are how a plant or animal answers to stimuli.
- All responses, together, produce behavior.

### 22-3. Simple behavior

The simplest living things are those which do not have specialized parts. Of course, their responses will show simple behavior. The behavior of protozoa, described above, is one example. A spider's web-spinning or a bird's nest-building are more complicated. And compared to the behavior of a trained monkey, seal, or dog, these activities are still simple. Compared to human behavior, these trained animal responses are also very simple.

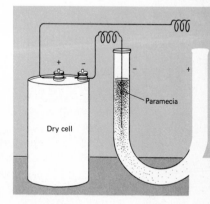

**Fig. 145-1**
How are the paramecia responding to the electrical current?

### 22-4. Plants show simple responses

**Fig. 145-2**
A trained horse clears a jump. How does this behavior differ from the retreat of protozoa from acid?

Do you remember what green plants need for growth? Yes, they need water and light. Their roots respond to water. Their leaves respond to light. Actually, these responses are simple and slow. There are no nerves in plants. The response is only a matter of growth.

The sensitive *mimosa* plant folds its leaves at the slightest touch.

Only a few kinds of plants show very quick movements. For example, the *Venus's-flytrap* snaps shut when an insect is so "foolish" as to enter its flower.

But most plants that have roots, stems, and leaves, show slower growth responses called TROPISMS (TROH-piz-umz). These types of responses are controlled by natural growth chemicals called AUXINS (AWK-sinz).

## Do and Discover

Investigation 15: How can we show tropisms in plants?

**Procedures**

1. Use a plant such as a geranium. Water as often as necessary.
2. Set up each experiment as in A and B.
3. Set up a box as shown in Figure C. It may be made of wood or cardboard, like a shoe box.

**Observations and Analysis**

1. Which way do roots grow? Which way do stems grow?
2. What *two* stimuli control root growth?
3. How do you know that the leaves in Figure C are responding to light, and not to air?

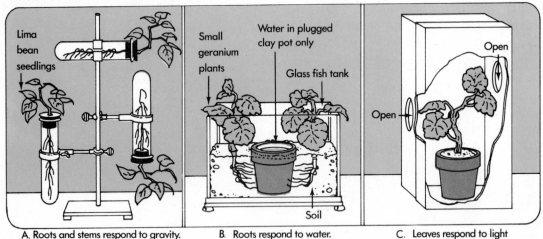

A. Roots and stems respond to gravity.   B. Roots respond to water.   C. Leaves respond to light

**Fig. 146-1**

22-5. Receiving the stimulus, giving the response

When your finger touches a sharp object, your arm muscle pulls the finger away. When your nose smells food, your salivary glands produce saliva. It all begins with a sense organ and ends in a muscle or a gland. The chart on page 147 shows the simple plan.

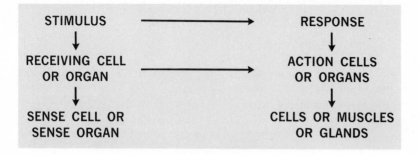

STIMULUS ⟶ RESPONSE
↓ ↓
RECEIVING CELL ⟶ ACTION CELLS
OR ORGAN OR ORGANS
↓ ↓
SENSE CELL OR CELLS OR MUSCLES
SENSE ORGAN OR GLANDS

## Learned So Far . . .

- Simple growth responses in plants are called tropisms.
- A stimulus is received by a cell or sense organ. A response is carried out by cells, muscles, or glands.

### 22-6. The senses of simple animals

How does an insect like a grasshopper know you are trying to catch it? Look at Figure 147-1. Locate the feelers or AN-TENNAE (an-TEN-ee). They are for touching and smelling. The grasshopper has three simple eye spots. It also has two compound eyes which contain hundreds of little lenses. No wonder the grasshopper is so sensitive!

Earthworms are also sensitive to their surroundings. Earthworms have light-sensitive spots. They feel moisture and chemicals with their skins. Earthworms, clams, lobsters, and insects do not really have brains. They have nerve bunches which receive stimuli and control responses.

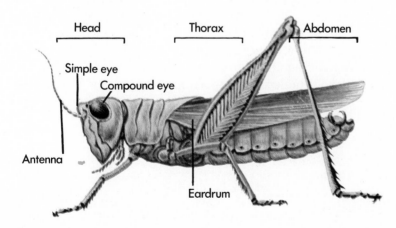

Head    Thorax    Abdomen

Simple eye
Compound eye

Antenna

Eardrum

**Fig. 147-1**

How is the grasshopper sensitive to its environment?

## Do and Discover

Investigation 16: How do insects respond to light?

### Procedures

1. Place several fruit flies into a test tube. Put a stopper in the open end. Fit the black sleeve over the left end of the tube.
2. Go into a dark room. Wait five minutes. Shine a flashlight at the clear end. Observe. Turn off the light.
3. Move the black sleeve to the right. Wait five minutes. Shine your flashlight on the clear end. Observe.
4. Cover the flashlight with yellow cellophane. Now repeat the experiment. What happens?

### Observations and Analysis

1. Record your observations.
2. What is the response? What kind is it?
3. What advantage is this response to the survival of the insects?

4. How is this response used in building insect traps?
5. Why would you turn off the lights in an open room to get the insects to leave?

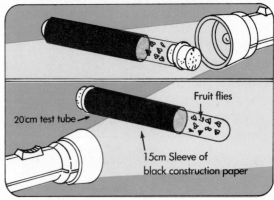

20 cm test tube
Fruit flies
15cm Sleeve of black construction paper

**Fig. 148-1**

**Fig. 148-2**

The antennae (an-TEN-ee) of a moth are its "feelers." They may lead a male moth to a female that is seven kilometers away! Antennae provide a sense of smell and direction.

### 22-7. Released chemicals in insects

Why do bees follow other bees to flowers? Why do female cockroaches follow a male cockroach just before mating? How do ants know where to go to find the sugar that a returning ant has found?

The answer is chemical. The chemicals released are called PHEROMONES (FER-uh-mohnz). It has been found that roaches, bees, and ants leave trails by releasing chemicals to which the others are sensitive.

There are now insect traps on the market which make use of this idea. Female pheromones, loaded into a trap, attract thousands of males. An important advantage is that pheromones are natural chemicals and do not pollute our environment.

### Learned So Far . . .

- Responses are necessary for life activities.
- Insects, protozoa, and earthworms show simple responses.

## 22-8. Chemical responses in humans

You've been frightened by a loud noise or a strange sight. Your heart responds by beating rapidly. Your face feels flushed. Your palms begin to sweat. This is the famous "fight or flight" response. Your body has a burst of energy to "fight" or run away from the stimulus.

How does this happen? Look at Figure 149-1. Find the ADRENAL (uh-DREEN-ul) GLANDS. They are on top of the kidneys. When you are frightened a message goes to your adrenal glands. They give off a chemical called ADRENA-LINE (uh-DREN-uh-lin). Adrenaline flows through the blood to its "target," the liver. The liver releases sugar to provide the extra energy needed. It also speeds up circulation.

Adrenaline is an example of a HORMONE (HOR-mohn). Our bodies produce many kinds of hormones. They are complicated chemicals that control special body functions. Hormones are produced in glands and released into the bloodstream. Then they travel to a special "target."

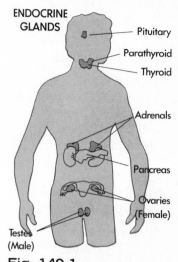

**Fig. 149-1**

The endocrine (EN-duh-krin) glands secret hormones. The diagram shows the major endocrine glands.

---

## SELF-STUDY GUIDE FOR CHAPTER 22

All answers should be written in your notebook. Please do not write in this book.

### Understanding the reading

A. *Find the Answers*
Write the letter of the correct answer.
1. What is the main idea of Chapter 22?
   a. Living things receive stimuli and produce responses.
   b. Insects know when there is light.
   c. Tropisms are good for plants.
   d. Crabs and lobsters are like other animals in their responses.
2. Earthworms feel moisture through
   a. nerves.
   b. skin.
   c. eyes.
   d. feet.
3. A moth flying to a candle
   a. is an example of a pheromone.
   b. is responding to heat.
   c. can happen only in the summer.
   d. is responding to light.
4. Bunches of nerves substitute for a brain in
   a. ameba.
   b. lobsters.
   c. plants.
   d. frogs.

B. *Locate the Idea*
Find the section in which each of these questions is answered. Write the number of the section and one or two sentences that answer the question.
1. What is a stimulus?
2. How do tropisms help plants in their needs for life?
3. What are the *feelers* of a cockroach?
4. What is a sense organ?

## Word tools

Unscramble the groups of letters to form science words. Read the first letters downward. They will spell the name of a musical instrument.

1. R O M T I P S (simple response)
2. O R O S T (absorbs water for plants)
3. R U I E N (waste formed by kidneys)
4. S C U M L E (biceps)
5. R P M A C U A E I M (protozoan)
6. R E P E I M X N T E (what you do in a lab)
7. S E U I T S (group of cells)

1. __ __ __ __ __ __ __
2. __ __ __ __ __
3. __ __ __ __ __
4. __ __ __ __ __ __
5. __ __ __ __ __ __ __ __ __ __
6. __ __ __ __ __ __ __ __ __ __
7. __ __ __ __ __ __

## Knowing what and why

A.  Do You Agree or Disagree?
    Write a sentence stating your reasons.
    1. Pheromones in insect traps should be opposed by "friends of the environment."
    2. It is easy to study the brain of an earthworm.
    3. Roots of plants respond to only one stimulus.
    4. Living things respond only to nonliving stimuli. (Hint: Look back to Chapter 4 to review nonliving factors.)

B.  Understanding the Diagrams
    Study Investigation 16. Answer the questions below.
    1. Why do you do the experiment in a dark room?
    2. Why do you move the sleeve back and forth?
    Look back to Figure 146-1.
    3. Do you need moisture in the test tubes in Figure A? Why?
    4. Does it matter whether the experiment in Figure C is done in the dark? Explain.
    5. In Figure B, what will the stems do? Why?

C.  What's the Difference?
    In a sentence or two, explain the difference between the two words in each pair.
    1. pheromones–photosynthesis
    2. stimulus–response
    3. tropism–auxin
    4. organ–system

## Looking further

1. Visit a seafood store. Examine lobsters, shrimps, and crabs to locate eyes and antennae.
2. On a dark, warm night, use a flashlight to attract insects. Use it uncovered first. Then use the flashlight covered with yellow, blue, and red cellophane. Does the color make a difference? Write your results.

## chapter 23

**TARGET**     **How are sense organs built to receive sensations?**

# *How sense organs receive sensations*

### 23-1 How many sense organs?

You know that we have five senses. Perhaps you have heard someone talk of a "sixth" sense. How many senses are there? How are they built? What can they do? As you might suspect, human sense organs are very well developed. But many "lower" animals have sense organs very much like ours.

### 23-2. Light—Form—Color

A puzzle: What receives the stimulus of light, can tell shades of light and can tell form, shape, size, depth, distance, and color? The human eye, of course. It is one of the most amazing "machines." Figure 152-1 shows its structure.

Light enters the eye through the opening called the *pupil* (2) and passes through the transparent *lens* (4). The object is "photographed" and forms an image on the RETINA (RET-uh-nuh) (5). The retina is made of tiny light-sensitive cells. The image formed is tiny, of course, and it is upside down! The little cells are connected to nerves in the retina. Some of these receive only white light. Others receive color. The nerves bunch together to form the OPTIC NERVE (6) which sends the message into your brain.

When the message gets to your brain you "see" the object right side up. The front of the eye is a transparent tissue

OPTOMETRIST (op-TOM-ih-trist): A trained person who tests vision with instruments to find eye defects and then prescribes glasses.
OPTICIAN (op-TISH-un): A person trained to grind lenses but not licensed to do eye examinations.
OPHTHALMOLOGIST (OF-thal-MOL-uh-jist): A physician (M.D.) who specializes in the function, diseases, and surgery of the eyes.

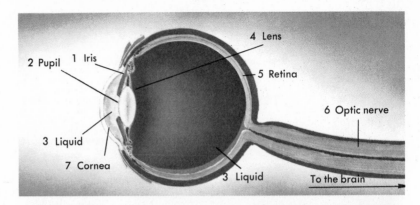

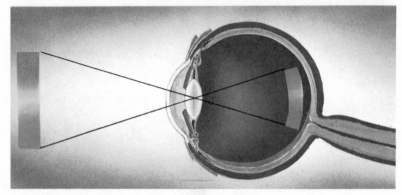

**Fig. 152-1**

A diagram of the human eye. Give the job of each part. The eye sees the image upside down. How does our brain get the view right?

called the CORNEA (KOR-nee-uh) (7). The cornea sometimes becomes diseased and causes blindness in some older people. Around the country, there are now *eye banks*. People sign a statement donating their eyes when they die. The healthy cornea is transplanted in the eye of the blind person whose sight usually returns.

**Fig. 152-2**

An optometrist examines a patient's retina with this machine.

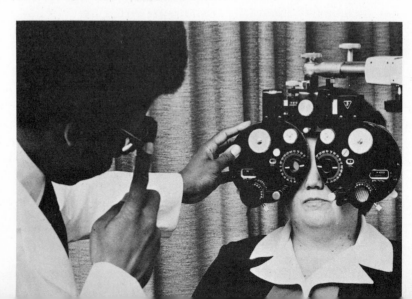

## 23-3. The functioning of the human eye

Some functions of the human eye can be studied with simple experiments. Other functions have been studied by dissection. Still others have been studied with complicated instruments.

## Do and Discover

**Investigation 17: What are some of the functions of the human eye?**

**Procedures**

1. Close your eyes. Wait about five minutes and then enter an absolutely dark closet. Open your eyes. What do you see?
2. In a lighted room, look at your eyes in a mirror. What color are they? Compare the color with your friend's eye color. What color do you see?
3. Get a friend to help you with this experiment. Stand a bright table lamp (without a shade) in front of you. Arrange it in such a way that when you snap it on, it will shine directly into your eyes. Stand in front of a mirror in a dark room for about five minutes. Now tell your friend to turn on the light. Continue to watch your pupil but have your friend turn the light away from you. What is happening now?

**Observations and Analysis**

1. Explain your results in step 1.
2. Which part of the eye is colored?
3. What kind of action is shown in step 3?

When there was a lot of light, your pupil contracted or got smaller. When the light was turned away and there was less light, your pupil got larger to allow more light to enter the eye. Your pupil gets smaller or larger according to how much light your eye needs in order to see. What is the advantage of this response?

> Some people are born ALBI-NOS (al-BY-nohz). They have no pigment in their eyes (nor in their skins or hair). They blink very sharply in ordinary light.

## Learned So Far . . .

- The amount of light causes a change in the size of the pupil.
- The *iris* is the colored part of the eye.
- The color and shape of an image is formed in the brain.

## 23-4. For hearing

When your dog is listening to something, you notice that its ears straighten or perk up. When you want to hear better, you may cup your hand and place it behind your ear. Both you and your dog are catching sound vibrations. Sound enters the outer ear (1) and moves through the tube (2) into the middle ear (3). The EARDRUM (4) and hearing bones (5) vibrate (move) at the same speed as the original sound. The vibration is passed into the hearing organ (6) in the inner ear (7). Then the AUDITORY (AW-dih-tohr-ee) NERVE (8) sends the stimulus into the brain. Your brain can interpret loudness, tone, and pitch.

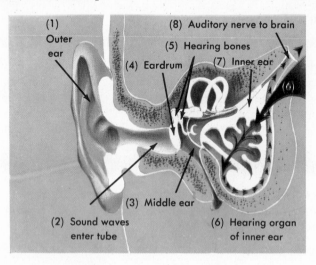

**Fig. 154-1**

The ear is the organ of sound and balance.

### 23-5. Why don't bats crash into walls?

In 1793 an Italian biologist named LAZZARO SPALLANZANI (LAD-dzah-roh spal-lun-ZAH-nee) became interested in the habits of bats. Bats are furry animals with very small and very poor eyes. They stay hidden by day and fly at night. You would expect them to have good eyes. Not so! You may have heard the expression, "blind as a bat."

Bats are supposed to be almost blind, thought Spallanzani. Why don't they crash into walls or into each other? How could they fly so accurately? Spallanzani got an idea. He caught some bats and plugged up their ears. Just as he had thought, the bats began to crash into each other and into walls. Spallanzani had solved the problem! Bats really guide themselves with their ears. But how?

The answer came years later. Scientists discovered that bats let out high-pitched screams. These sounds are more than six times higher than the highest sounds human ears can hear. Screams from bats hit walls, trees, or other bats and are bounced back as echoes. The bats hear these echoes and steer away from the walls or the trees.

Human Hearing: 20-20,000 vibrations per second or *hertz*

Dog Hearing: 20-30,000 vps or hertz

Bat Hearing: up to 150,000 vps or hertz

### 23-6. For balance

Do your ears ever feel funny when you come down in an elevator too fast? If they do, it is because the air pressure in the middle ear has suddenly become unbalanced from the air pressure in your outer ear. What do you do? You swallow hard. This forces a bubble of air through the tube (7) into the middle ear. Now the pressure is balanced and you feel normal again.

How do you know when you are lying down, leaning to one side, or standing on your head? Your ear is what gives you your sense of balance. The SEMICIRCULAR (sem-ih-SUR-kyoo-lur) CANALS in your ear (6) are filled with a fluid and tiny hairs. Your body position stimulates these canals and the message is sent out through the nerve into the brain.

## Learned So Far . . .

- The human ear receives sound.
- The ear also sends messages of balance and position to the brain.

### 23-7. What a taste!

Good or bad? Sweet or sour? Bitter or salty? *Taste* is a sense used to detect chemicals. Your tongue is covered with *taste buds*. The taste buds have tiny nerve endings in them. With each chemical a sensation is sent on to the brain. The surface of the tongue has been mapped out for tastes. Taste protects animals against poisonous food. In humans, taste gives enjoyment to food and improves digestion.

Bitter

Sour

Sweet

Salt

**Fig. 155-1**

Taste sensations in the tongue are in different parts.

## Do and Discover

Investigation 18: Which parts of the tongue taste what kinds of substances?

### Procedures
1. Make up separate solutions of salt, sugar, vinegar (sour), and a crushed aspirin tablet (bitter) in four test tubes.
2. Get 4 cotton swabs, one for each solution.
3. Touch different parts of the tongue with each solution. Rinse your mouth with clean sink water between tastes. Do the tests blindfolded.

### Observations and Analysis
1. If you did the tests right, your results should be the same as Figure 155-1. Make your own "map."
2. Why should you do the tests blindfolded?

### 23-8. What an odor!

Odors come to our noses through the air. The molecules of a substance drift into the nose and stimulate tiny nerve endings which send messages to the brain. How do we recognize an odor? The odors of strange materials can be described as strong, faint, pleasant, or bad. However, we can only recognize an odor by experience. Our sense of smell and our sense of taste are closely related. For example, if you pinch your nose closed and eat a piece of onion, the onion will taste as "flat" as a piece of potato. Try this also with an apple and a pear. What are the results of your experiments and why?

### 23-9. Sensations of the skin

It feels rough! It hurts! It's hot! It's cold! Here you have the four separate SENSATIONS (sen-SAY-shunz) of the skin: *touch, pain, heat,* and *cold.* You can map these areas very easily.

When a housefly is walking on something, it is really "tasting" with its feet! Sharks can detect as little as one drop of blood in a million.

Fig. 156-1

These nerve endings from the nose of a rat are shown 7000 times their real size. What two senses do these cells help control?

## Do and Discover

### Procedures

A. To find out where some of the pain points are on the skin, do the following:
  1. Draw a square (2 cm by 2 cm) on the back of your hand with a ballpoint pen. Divide the square into sixteen squares (four squares by four squares).
  2. Using a sharp needle, locate the spots where you feel the pain. You will see that in some places the touch senses are closer together.
B. To find out where some of the heat and cold spots are on the skin, follow these steps:

  1. Prepare a square (as above) on the hand of a friend. Blindfold him or her.
  2. Heat a needle in hot water. Test the squares and ask your friend to repeat his or her feelings.
  3. Chill the needle over an ice cube. Do this test again.

### Observations and Analysis

1. What do you now know about "dead spots" on the skin?
2. Is this an advantage? Explain your answer.

Skin sensations are extremely important for protection. If your skin has no sensations, you find it hard to tell if you cut yourself, burn yourself, or even break bones. The sense organs are located in the skin. There, nerves pick up the sensations and send them to the brain.

## Learned So Far . . .

- The tongue has taste buds for different tastes on different parts of the tongue.
- The skin can sense touch, pain, heat, and cold.
- Smell is received by nerves in the nose.

## SELF-STUDY GUIDE FOR CHAPTER 23

All answers should be written in your notebook. Please do not write in this book.

### Understanding the reading

A. *Find the Answers*
Write the letter of the correct answer.
  1. What is the main idea of Chapter 23?
    a. We don't really hear until messages of sound go to our brain.
    b. Our sixth sense is poorly developed.
    c. Our sense organs are not perfect.
    d. Sense organs are complicated tissues specialized to receive stimuli.
  2. It may take a little time to know the taste of food because
    a. the material has to dissolve.
    b. the saliva masks the taste.

c. it takes a little time for the taste to spread over the tongue.
d. you must also smell the substance.
3. Images in the eye are formed
   a. upside down in the lens.
   b. right side up under the lid.
   c. upside down on the retina.
   d. upside down in the brain.
4. Between the outer and inner ear, you will find the
   a. organ of balance.
   b. hearing bones.
   c. eardrum.
   d. auditory nerve.

B. *Locate the Idea*
Find the section, figure, or margin note that answers the question. Write where the answer is found and one or two sentences that answer the question.
1. Where does the optic nerve receive stimuli?
2. How are albino eyes different from the usual eye?
3. Where does sound go *after* it goes through the bones of the middle ear?
4. Which animal can receive sound with the highest number of vibrations per second?

## Word tools

In a sentence, give the job of each part. Next to its job write the sense organ to which it belongs. Write all the answers in your notebook.
1. iris
2. pupil
3. auditory nerve
4. taste bud
5. retina
6. eardrum
7. optic nerve
8. lens

## Knowing what and why

A. *True or False?*
Write if the statement is true or false. Then explain your answer in one or two sentences.
1. Feeling a burn is really helpful to life.
2. The only function of the ear is for hearing.
3. It's hard to taste your food when you have a cold in the nose.
4. A person who loses his hearing can remember the tune of a song.
5. We "see" with our brains.
6. A needle's point may not always hurt your fingertip.

B. *Analyzing the Investigation*
Study Investigation 18. Answer the questions below.
1. Why do we use *small* cotton swabs?
2. Why is the person blindfolded?
3. Why do you rinse your mouth between tastes?
4. If you used saccharin and lemon juice and told your friend you were using sugar and vinegar, would he or she know the difference? Explain.

## chapter 24

**TARGET**    How is the nervous system built to do its work?

# *The structure of the nervous system*

## 24-1. Looking back . . .

Earlier, you learned that the nervous system, like all other systems, is made up of organs, tissues, and cells. Turn back to Figure 138-1. The neuron shown has one long branch and many short branches. These cells are very sensitive to stimuli. Some neurons have branches a full meter long!

## 24-2. Nerves reach out everywhere

Neurons form tissues which then form long, thin nerve fibers (threads). Like a huge telephone system, the nerve fibers spread out to form a network. Every part of the body is reached by nerve fibers to pick up the stimuli. But, what are nerves? They are really bundles of nerve fibers. They are put together like the wires inside a telephone cable. The nerves are held together by a covering of tissue.

> A human brain weighs from 1 to 1.5 kg. No!—The size of someone's brain has nothing to do with intelligence.

## 24-3. All together . . .

If the nerves shown in Fig. 160-1 were not connected to some central place, the body would really not have control. Your left leg would operate separately from your right leg. Your fingers would not work together. Grasping would be hard. There would be no COORDINATION (koh-or-duh-NAY-shun).

## 24-4. The central nervous system

Look at Fig. 160-1. You can see that all nerves are connected. We call this cord in which all the nerves are brought together the *spinal cord*. The spinal cord runs up and down the length of your backbone and enters the skull. It is protected from injury by a series of bones called VERTEBRAE (VUR-tuh-bree). Inside the skull, the nerve tissue forms a large organ, the *brain*.

Look at Fig. 161-1. The brain is made of three parts. The largest, wrinkled part is called the CEREBRUM (suh-REE-brum). The middle section is the CEREBELLUM (ser-uh-BEL-um). The lowest part is the MEDULLA OBLONGATA (mih-DUL-uh ob-lon-GAH-tuh). Along the spinal cord there are 31 pairs of spinal nerves that control different sections of the body below the neck. There are also 12 head nerves. Two examples of head nerves are the optic nerve from the eyes and the auditory nerve from the ears. These organs, the brain and spinal cord, make up the CENTRAL NERVOUS SYSTEM.

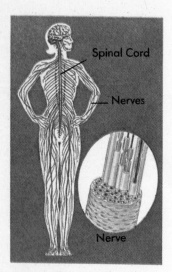

**Fig. 160-1**

Nerves connect all parts of the body to the brain and spinal cord. A nerve is a bundle of nerve fibers.

| CENTRAL NERVOUS SYSTEM | | |
|---|---|---|
| **Part** | **Function** | **What It Connects To** |
| Brain { —Cerebrum —Cerebellum —Medulla | Main Control Center | 12 pairs of head nerves |
| Spinal Cord | Switching Center | 31 pairs of nerves to the rest of the body |
| Nerves | "Cables and Wires" | Carry impulses to all parts of the body |

## 24-5. Which part does what?

How do we know the jobs of different parts of the central nervous system? Much of what we do know comes from studying injuries and disease. Farmers noticed long ago that if a chicken's head is cut off (brain removed), the chicken can run around for a short time. Running is therefore controlled by the spinal cord. A growth on one section of the brain, a *tumor*, might make the person lose his vision. So we found out that this part of the brain controls vision. Look at the "brain map" to give you an idea of where different functions are controlled in the brain.

## Learned So Far . . .

- Stimuli and responses are controlled by a central nervous system.
- The neuron cells make up nerve tissue to form nerves, the spinal cord, and the brain.
- The nerves, spinal cord, and brain make up the central nervous system.

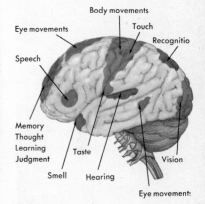

**Fig. 161-1**

**The spinal cord runs into the brain. How is the brain protected from injury? How is the spinal cord protected from injury?**

## 24-6. The simplest response of all

Idiots and geniuses, young and old, rich and poor, all have the same simple responses. We are all born with the ability to do these simple jobs. Otherwise, we could not stay alive. From the time you are a baby until you are very old, only sickness or injury can interfere with these simple acts.

How does a baby know how to swallow? How does a baby know how to pull its toe away from a safety pin left carelessly open? The answer is that we are born with certain simple responses. Simple inborn responses are called REFLEX (REE-fleks) acts, or just *reflexes*. Let's trace the path of a reflex in Figure 162-1.

## 24-7. What good are reflexes?

How long did it take to pull the finger away from the sharp pin? How long does it take for your eyelid to close when a speck of dust gets into your eye? These reflexes have been measured in laboratories. Some reflexes take as little as *one-sixth (1/6) of a second!* This is the chief benefit of a

**Fig. 161-2**

**What does the "brain map" locate?**

**Fig. 162-1**

Your fingertip has touched a sharp pinpoint. The message is carried along the nerve fiber into the spinal cord. There, the message "jumps" to another nerve fiber which carries the message out to the muscle of your arm. The muscle contracts. The arm is pulled away. Is the brain used? Explain.

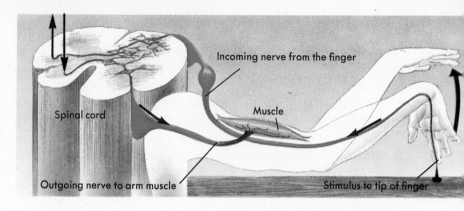

Incoming nerve from the finger

Spinal cord

Muscle

Outgoing nerve to arm muscle

Stimulus to tip of finger

reflex—it is fast. It is also automatic. It requires no thought. It does not have to be learned. Reflexes are the first line of defense against danger. Reflexes help you carry out your life functions. Does your brain also work in reflexes? Do you know when your finger is burned or cut? Of course! Your spinal cord tells this to your cerebrum. But your cerebrum learns this only *after* your finger has been pulled away.

| BEST KNOWN REFLEX ACTIONS ||
|---|---|
| **Stimulus** | **Reflex** |
| Dust in eye | Blinking of eyelids |
| Bright light | Closing of pupils |
| Loud noise | Jumping |
| Food in back of throat | Swallowing |
| Food odor and taste | Flow of saliva |
| Dust in nose | Sneezing |
| Cold skin | Shivering or goose pimples |

**Fig. 162-2**

The knee jerk is a reflex often tested by a doctor. Try it with your friend.

## Learned So Far . . .

- The simplest response is the reflex.
- Reflexes are inborn, involuntary, automatic, and fast.
- Reflexes need two nerves for completion.
- Reflexes become known to the brain, but after the response takes place.

### 24-8. Let's go to Florida

No, we are not talking about your family. We are talking about birds! Each year, as the weather grows cool, thousands of birds migrate to a warmer climate. How do they know the route? How do they know when and how to come back? How do Columbia River salmon know about swimming upstream to reach quiet waters in which to lay their eggs? African elephants follow the rain to find water. Most birds build very complicated nests. How do they know so much about building?

All of these acts are *inborn* and not learned. They are called INSTINCTS (IN-stinktz). Scientists believe that instincts may be a *whole chain of reflex actions*. Although this seems like very intelligent behavior, it is automatic.

**Fig. 163-1**
**What instincts keep these cheetahs together?**

## SELF-STUDY GUIDE FOR CHAPTER 24

All answers should be written in your notebook. Please do not write in this book.

*Understanding the reading*

A. *Find the Answers*
Write the letter of the correct answer.
1. Dust in the nose is a stimulus whose response is controlled by the
   a. nerves in the head.
   b. medulla.
   c. spinal cord.
   d. cerebellum.
2. A nerve is
   a. a nerve cell.
   b. many sensory cells.

c. a bundle of nerve fibers.
d. part of the retina.
3. Reflex actions are
   a. inborn and controlled by the brain.
   b. inborn and controlled by the spinal cord.
   c. automatic and learned.
   d. automatic, but controlled by the medulla.

B. *Locate the Idea*
Find the section in which each of the questions is answered. Write the number of the section and one or two sentences that answer the question.
1. Does the brain control reflex acts? Why or why not?
2. Where do reflex messages "link up"?
3. Is nest building by birds a reflex act?
4. What parts of the brain control heartbeat?

C. *Which One?*
In the following groups of words find the "umbrella" word: the one word which *includes* the other three.

Example: penny, coin, dime, nickel: *coin*
1. reflex, instinct, behavior, stimulus
2. brain, cerebrum, medulla, cerebellum
3. organism, brain, neuron, nerve
4. plasma, platelet, red cells, blood

## Knowing what and why

A. *True or False?*
Write if the statement is true or false. Then explain your answers in one or two sentences.
1. Shivering in a cold room is a useful response.
2. A blood clot anywhere in the cerebrum will make the person forget everything they ever knew.
3. The optic nerve brings stimuli to the spinal cord.
4. A genius responds faster than a mentally retarded person to dust in the nose.

B. *Number, Please . . .*
Supply the correct number. Write it in your notebook.
1. Number of head nerves.
2. Number of spinal nerves.
3. Number of parts to brain.
4. Time for a reflex act.

C. *Using Your Judgment*
Which is a stimulus? Which is a response? In your notebook, separate these into two lists, one for *stimuli* and one for *responses*. Where there is a *response* write a *stimulus* that might have caused it.
1. smell of vinegar
2. alarm clock ring
3. leaves grow toward sunlight
4. bright spotlight
5. shivering
6. odor of roses
7. Venus's-flytrap closes
8. cat runs to milk plate
9. squirrel sits up tall
10. feather on skin

## Looking further

In an encyclopedia, look up *sleep*. Write a report that answers these questions:
a. What is sleep?
b. What are dreams?
c. What is REM (rapid eye movement)?

## chapter 25

**TARGET**    How do we change our responses for intelligent behavior?

# *The responses of learning*

### 25-1. Educating your pets

Your cat has learned to go to the door and "meow" when it wants to go out. Your dog will give you its paw when you put out your hand. Squirrels in the park will sit up on their hind legs when you hold out a nut. Do you keep tropical fish? Tap the fish tank. Then drop some food on the surface of the water. Continue this for 10 or 12 days. Now tap the tank and the fish will come to the top *before* you give them food. You now have "educated" fish! How does this happen?

### 25-2. Pavlov trains the dogs

IVAN PAVLOV (PAV-lov), a Russian scientist, wanted to know how animals learned certain reactions. In 1897 he began a number of simple experiments. These experiments tested a dog's response to particular stimuli.

When a dog sees and smells food, its salivary glands flow. It drools at the mouth. The stimulus is smell. Saliva flow is a reflex. Could this inborn reflex be changed? One of Pavlov's experiments with dogs showed it could.

Each time Pavlov gave a dog some food, he rang a bell. The dog drooled. Pavlov measured the amount of saliva. The experiment went on for many days. Each time he gave food to

**Fig. 166-1**

The porpoise has been conditioned to take fish from its trainer's mouth.

the dog he rang the bell and saliva flowed. One day, Pavlov was ready for the big question. He brought no food. He rang the bell and the dog drooled anyway! What had happened? Pavlov had substituted a new stimulus (the bell) for the old stimulus (smell). The response was the same! Pavlov had changed the conditions of the act. He had developed a CONDITIONED (kun-DISH-und) REFLEX.

### 25-3. Conditioning is one kind of learning

PSYCHOLOGY (sy-KOL-uh-jee) is the branch of science that studies behavior. Many PSYCHOLOGISTS (sy-KOL-uh-jists) believe that one way of learning is by *conditioning*. We learn to play ball by setting up certain paths to our brains. We condition our eyes to look for the ball. We place our bodies a certain way and swing the bat just right to hit the ball. When we hear the thud of the ball on the bat, we take off for first base. In the same way, conditioning is used in animal training. Trainers use rewards such as food or petting to get the animal to respond the right way.

### Learned So Far . . .

- In a conditioned reflex, we substitute a new stimulus for the old one. The response remains the same.
- Animals and humans use conditioning for some of their learning.

**Fig. 166-2**

This chimp is learning sign language from his trainer. What kind of learning is this?

### 25-4. Learning by thinking

Conditioned learning is only one of the ways we learn. Thinking is also a way that we learn to do things. Thinking involves actively using our brain. Thinking means that we form ideas or patterns in our mind. The chief center in the brain for this kind of learning is the cerebrum. However, thinking also involves other activities. For example, when we learn to type, we first use our eyes to see the keys and our ears to hear the rhythm. We use our sense of touch to locate the keys. But, we do more than that. We use our muscles to sit up and balance our bodies. This means that we are also using our cerebellums.

Learning by thinking also uses something called JUDGMENT (JUJ-munt). Judgment means that you make a choice. Do you slip the paper into the typewriter halfway or a quarter of the way? Do you set your margins at one inch or two inches? Do you set the type single-space or double-space? These are all matters of judgment.

## 25-5. Learning by imitation

Imitation is another way we learn. This is a method that involves repeating an action that we have seen other people do. For instance, when you were learning to ride a bike, you saw a friend or an older brother or sister riding down the street. You saw how they were sitting and pedaling. So you got on your bike and tried to do the same thing. You learned to ride the bike by imitation.

Learning also requires *memory*. The last time you went to the store for your mother, you walked two blocks and then crossed the street. This time you *remember* the way you went before. You have now learned your way to the store!

## 25-6. Trial and error

Figure 167-1 shows a *maze*. It is used very often to show how an animal learns. At the left door is a white rat. At the right door is a piece of cheese. The rat smells the cheese. The rat must then find the way to get it. Quite often it comes to a blind alley. It must turn around and go back. But after a few trials and a few errors, the rat learns to find the cheese faster. Many of us learn things just this way, by trial and error. Now you know how we got the old saying, "Practice makes perfect."

Learning is a very complicated job. But it also takes practice. In other words, you have to learn how to learn!

## 25-7. What is intelligence?

The simple definition of intelligence is the ability to learn. To learn what? To learn anything. Is everyone intelligent? Yes, but there are differences. Except for a very small number, all people can learn. We also know that some people learn some things better than others. We say they have special APTITUDES (AP-tih-toodz). For example, some people are very quick in learning to fix a car or work a sewing machine. Some people can learn to play the piano while

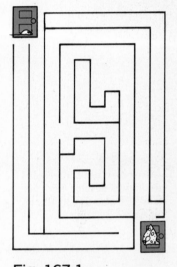

**Fig. 167-1**

The rat uses trial and error to find the cheese. It gets faster and faster the more tries it makes. The same thing happens when you do a jigsaw puzzle over and over again.

others cannot. Some people are very good in arithmetic and some in drawing. Some people can write poetry or figure out a deal in business.

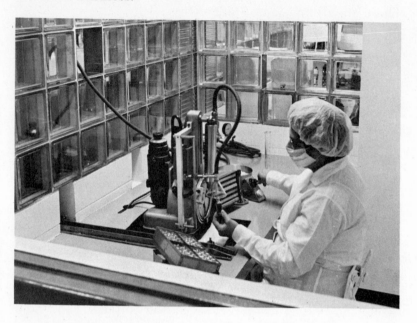

**Fig. 168-1**

This woman used intelligent learning to develop her skill. Does she also use habits in her work?

### 25-8. Learning to learn

Learning uses many skills, not just one. If you are learning to drive, you are also using the skill of reading road signs. Reading is a skill you learned before. If you are learning to be a waiter, you are using the skill of adding up the check, a skill you learned before. Learning means putting many skills together to build a new skill.

---

**ELEMENTS OF INTELLIGENCE**

**Reasoning:**
"If I go home now, I'll avoid the rain."

**Memory:**
"Next period I have gym."

**Judgment:**
"This bread is 65¢ for one pound. This one is $1.20 for two pounds. The second bread is cheaper."

---

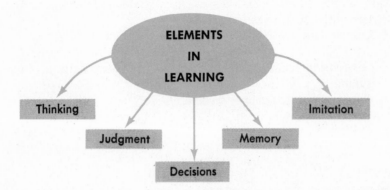

Fig. 169-1

## 25-9. It's a habit

Can you tie your shoe laces while you are listening to the radio? Of course. Tying your shoe laces is a *habit*. It took you a long time to learn how to tie those laces. You had to watch carefully to figure out how to do it. You used trial and error and finally got it. Then you speeded it up. Now you can do it with your eyes closed. Habits are a little like reflexes. They are automatic and you don't have to think about them. But there is a big difference. You were not born with habits. You learned them and you can break them.

Are habits good for you? Yes, if they are *good* habits. Imagine if you had to figure out every day how to walk to school or how to hold your pencil or how to tie a lace or how to brush your teeth. Your cerebrum would be so busy, you could never learn anything new!

## 25-10. Some deadly habits

There are habits that are helpful to us. But there are other habits which can be dangerous—even deadly. For example, smoking cigarettes has been linked to lung disease, including cancer. Drinking a lot of alcoholic beverages may be harmful. Even drinking too much coffee which contains CAFFEINE (KAF-een) may not be good for you.

A far more dangerous habit is the abuse of harmful drugs. The best way to avoid a habit that can hurt you is not to start.

## Learned So Far . . .

- Learning uses the cerebrum.
- Learning involves conditioning, imitation, thinking, and trial and error.
- Learning is voluntary. It includes memory, judgment, and reasoning.
- Habits are unconscious, involuntary acts that you once had to learn.

## PROFILE OF A GREAT SCIENTIST　　Konrad Lorenz

What do baby ducks or baby geese do as soon as they are born? They follow their mother wherever she goes! And they usually stay with their "brothers and sisters." How do they know? Years ago, Konrad Lorenz, an Austrian biologist, became interested in this question.

Konrad Lorenz
1904–

He divided a newly-laid group of duck eggs, placing half in an incubator, leaving the other half with the mother duck. The newly-hatched ducklings in the nest followed the mother. The incubator ducklings followed Lorenz. In fact, he found that newly-hatched birds would follow almost any moving object they saw *early enough* in their lives: a toy bird, a moving box, a balloon.

What does this mean? According to Lorenz, animals are born with "fixed" behavior patterns such as following their mother. Then, early in life, new patterns are learned from whomever the animals have followed. Lorenz called this process IMPRINTING (im-PRIN-ting).

Other scientists, since Lorenz, have explained that imprinting can explain how animals behave in relation to each other. For example, female monkeys raised without mothers or brothers and sisters, have refused to care for their young.

Lorenz is considered the father of the behavioral science, called ETHOLOGY (ee-THOL-uh-jee). In 1973 he received (with two other scientists) the Nobel Prize in Medicine and Physiology.

## SELF-STUDY GUIDE FOR CHAPTER 25

All answers should be written in your notebook. Please do not write in this book.

### Understanding the reading _____

A. *Find the Answers*
   Write the letter of the correct answer.
   1. Which type of learning did Pavlov study?
      a. habit
      b.. imitation
      c. conditioned reflex
      d. trial and error
   2. We learn a new skill like driving by
      a. setting up new stimuli.
      b. using our reasoning.
      c. coordinating various different skills.
      d. conditioning our reflexes.
   3. A trained chimpanzee shows intelligence
      a. by learning.
      b. by developing instincts.
      c. through better use of its spinal nerves.
      d. by conditioning with food.

   4. Habits are
      a. automatic and learned.
      b. automatic and inborn.
      c. automatic and dangerous.
      d. just a better kind of instinct.

B. *True or False*
   Write *true* if the statement is true. If the statement is false, change the word in *italics* to make the statement true.
   1. In a conditioned reflex, we substitute a new *response* for the old one.
   2. Trial and *judgment* is the way that a rat learns to run through a maze.
   3. We learn many things, such as riding a bike, by *imitation.*
   4. Inborn automatic responses are *habits.*
   5. The ability to learn is *intelligence.*

### Word tools _____

Match the terms from *Column B* with those in *Column A.* (Two terms will not be used.)

**Column A**
1. nest building by wasps
2. nerve cell
3. imprinted behavior
4. vertebrae
5. Pavlov's work
6. ability

**Column B**
a. conditioning
b. aptitude
c. medulla
d. instinct
e. optic nerve
f. spinal cord
g. neuron
h. Lorenz

## Knowing what and why

A.  *True or False?*
    Write if the statement is true or false. Then explain your answers in one or two sentences.
    1. Animals use trial and error in learning more than reasoning.
    2. Pavlov's dogs could never be normal again.
    3. An expert truck driver, in a different job for ten years, will be just as good when he returns to his old job.
    4. Homework for students is really of no use.

B.  *Understanding the Diagram*
    In your notebook number from 1 to 6. Next to each number write the name of the part labelled on the diagram. Next to its name write the chief function of that part.

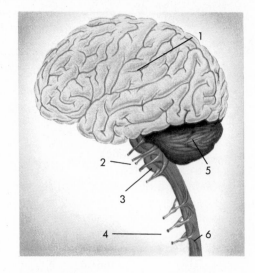

**Fig. 172-1**

## Looking further

1. Set up a conditioning experiment for your dog, cat, or other pet.
   a. State clearly what you want to accomplish.
   b. State how you will do it.
   c. Keep notes of your progress.
2. Arrange to have a conversation with the music teacher and typing teacher in your school. Ask them to explain how they find habit-forming useful in developing instrumental and typing skills.
3. Review in your mind some bad habits that you have. Think out a program to break these bad habits. *Start today!*
4. In a reference book, find out about the recent experiments done on the intelligence of *dolphins.*

# Appendix

## Conversion Tables for Metric and English Systems

English to Metric | | Metric to English | |

──────────────── Length ────────────────

| To convert | Multiply by | To convert | Multiply by |
|---|---|---|---|
| in. to mm | 25.40 | mm to in. | 0.04 |
| in. to cm | 2.54 | cm to in. | 0.39 |
| ft. to m | 0.30 | m to ft. | 3.28 |
| yd. to m | 0.91 | m to yd. | 1.09 |
| mi. to km | 1.61 | km to mi. | 0.62 |

──────────────── Area ────────────────

| | | | |
|---|---|---|---|
| sq. in. to sq. cm | 6.45 | sq. cm to sq. in. | 0.15 |
| sq. ft. to sq. m | 0.09 | sq. m to sq. ft. | 10.76 |
| sq. yd. to sq. m | 0.84 | sq. m to sq. yd. | 1.20 |
| a. to ha | 0.41 | ha to a. | 2.46 |
| sq. mi. to sq. km | 2.59 | sq. km to sq. mi. | 0.39 |

──────────────── Volume ────────────────

| | | | |
|---|---|---|---|
| cu. in. to cc | 16.39 | cc to cu. in. | 0.06 |
| cu. ft. to cu. m | 0.03 | cu. m to cu. ft. | 35.31 |
| cu. yd. to cu. m | 0.76 | cu. m to cu. yd. | 1.31 |

──────────────── Capacity (liquid) ────────────────

| | | | |
|---|---|---|---|
| fl. oz. to mL | 30.00 | mL to fl. oz. | 0.34 |
| fl. oz. to L | 0.03 | L to fl. oz. | 33.81 |
| qt. to L | 0.95 | L to qt. | 1.06 |
| gal. to L | 3.78 | L to gal. | 0.26 |

──────────────── Mass (weight) ────────────────

| | | | |
|---|---|---|---|
| oz. avdp. to g | 28.35 | g to oz. avdp. | 0.03 |
| lb. avdp. to kg | 0.45 | kg to lb. avdp. | 2.21 |
| ton to t | 0.91 | t to ton | 1.10 |

## Abbreviations

English | | Metric | |

| | | | |
|---|---|---|---|
| a. - acre(s) | lb. - pound(s) | cc - cubic centimeter(s) | kg - kilogram(s) |
| avdp. - avoirdupois | mi. - mile(s) | cm - centimeter(s) | L - liter(s) |
| ft. - foot, feet | oz. - ounce(s) | cu. - cubic | m - meter(s) |
| gal. - gallon(s) | qt. - quart(s) | g - gram(s) | mm - millimeter(s) |
| fl. oz. - fluid ounce(s) | sq. - square | ha - hectare(s) | t - metric ton(s) |
| in. - inch(es) | yd. - yard(s) | | |

# Glossary

| | | |
|---|---|---|
| absorb | (ab-SORB) | to take in; example: lung tissue absorbs oxygen |
| adaptation | (ad-up-TAY-shun) | an organism's ability to adapt to its environment |
| adrenaline | (uh-DREN-uh-lin) | a hormone produced by the adrenal gland; controls the emergency release of energy |
| albinos | (al-BY-nohz) | pure white animals with pink eyes; mutations that occur in plants as well as animals |
| alcoholism | (AL-kuh-ho-liz-um) | an abnormal dependence on alcohol |
| algae | (AL-jee) | microscopic one-celled green plants |
| ameba | (uh-MEE-buh) | microscopic one-celled animal that changes its shape |
| antennae | (an-TEN-ee) | feelers on the heads of insects that are used for touching and smelling |
| aquatic | (uh-KWAT-ik) | living or growing in or near water |
| assimilation | (uh-sim-uh-LAY-shun) | life process by which plants and animals change food into living matter |
| astronauts | (AS-truh-nots) | people who travel in space |
| astronomy | (uh-STRON-uh-mee) | the study of the stars, planets, and other heavenly bodies |
| atmosphere | (AT-muh-sfeer) | the gaseous envelope that surrounds the earth |
| auditory | (AW-dih-tohr-ee) | having to do with hearing |
| auxins | (AWK-sinz) | compounds in plants which control tropisms |
| bathyscaphe | (BATH-ih-skayf) | a type of research submarine that can dive to the ocean's floor |
| behavior | (bih-HAY-vyur) | the way in which an organism responds to its environment |
| biceps | (BY-ceps) | the large muscle at the front of the upper arm |
| binoculars | (buh-NOK-yuh-lurz) | field glasses which enlarge objects at a distance |
| biologist | (by-OL-uh-jist) | scientist who studies living things |
| biology | (by-OL-uh-jee) | the science of life |
| biome | (BY-ohm) | large area of land or water in which plants and animals form a balanced system within the environment |

174

| | | |
|---|---|---|
| biosphere | (BY-uh-sfeer) | the zone surrounding the earth which forms the home of living things |
| botany | (BOT-uh-nee) | the branch of biology that studies plant life |
| calcium | (KAL-see-um) | a soft white metallic element that is an essential part of bones |
| cambium | (KAM-bee-um) | the growing tissue in plants |
| carcinogens | (kar-SIN-uh-junz) | cancer-causing substances |
| cartilage | (KAR-tuh-lij) | flexible, supportive tissue that connects bones and also forms parts of the skeleton |
| cellulose | (SEL-yuh-lohs) | nonliving compound contained in cell walls |
| Celsius | (SEL-see-us) | centigrade temperature |
| centimeter | (SEN-tuh-mee-tur) | measure of length |
| centrifuge | (SEN-truh-fyooj) | a machine that spins its contents to remove moisture and to separate liquids at different densities |
| cerebellum | (ser-uh-BEL-um) | the middle section of the brain |
| cerebrum | (suh-REE-brum) | part of the brain that controls conscious voluntary acts |
| chemistry | (KEM-ih-stree) | the science that concerns itself with the structure, properties, and composition of matter |
| chlorophyll | (KLOR-uh-fil) | compound in green plant cells which controls food-making |
| chloroplasts | (KLOR-uh-plasts) | the part of the plant cell where chlorophyll is stored |
| cilia | (SIL-ee-uh) | hairlike structures found on some plant and animal cells |
| circulation | (sur-kyuh-LAY-shun) | movement of the blood through the body |
| conditioned | (kun-DISH-und) | animals taught to react in a certain desired way by substituting new stimulus for an old one |
| coordination | (koh-or-duh-NAY-shun) | ability to use different parts of the body at the same time |
| cornea | (KOR-nee-uh) | the clear covering of the lens and iris of the eye |
| cosmic rays | (KOZ-mik) | electromagnetic rays from the atmosphere |
| cytoplasm | (SY-tuh-plazum) | living matter in a cell outside the nucleus |

| | | |
|---|---|---|
| data | (DAY-tuh) | a collection of figures and factual information |
| decomposers | (dee-kum-POH-zurz) | plants and animals which break down living material for nutrition |
| dehydrated | (dee-HY-drayt-ed) | the removal of water from any substance |
| diabetes | (dy-uh-BEE-teez) | a disorder caused by the failure of the pancreas to produce insulin |
| digestion | (dih-JES-chun) | chemical change in the molecules for food absorption |
| dissection | (dy-SEK-shun) | to cut something apart for study |
| ecology | (ih-KOL-uh-jee) | the study of the relationships between living things and their environments |
| emphysema | (em-fih-SEE-muh) | a lung disease sometimes caused by excessive smoking |
| epidermis | (ep-ih-DUR-mis) | the outer layer of tissue in plants or skin |
| epithelial | (ep-uh-THEE-lee-ul) | tissue that covers and protects the surface of an organism |
| ethology | (ee-THOL-uh-jee) | the study of animal behavior within given environments |
| excretion | (ik-SKREE-shun) | elimination of body waste |
| famine | (FAM-in) | a widespread lack of food through which many starve |
| fertilizers | (FUR-tuh-ly-zurz) | organic or inorganic substance applied to soil to feed plants |
| fluoroscope | (FLOOR-uh-skohp) | a kind of x-ray machine used to view the organs and bones on a screen |
| fungi | (FUN-jy) | plants without chlorophyll, such as molds and mushrooms |
| geology | (jee-OL-uh-jee) | the study of the earth's crust |
| germinate | (JUR-muh-nayt) | sprout; to grow from a seed into a plant |
| gestation | (jeh-STAY-shun) | the length of time of a pregnancy |
| hectare | (HEK-tair) | metric system measure equal to 10,000 square meters |
| hemoglobin | (HEE-muh-gloh-bin) | the iron compound found in red blood cells |
| heredity | (huh-RED-ih-tee) | the passing on of characteristics from parents to offspring through the genes |
| heroin | (HER-oh-in) | a habit-forming drug made from morphine |
| hibernation | (hy-bur-NAY-shun) | to sleep through the winter as bears and some other animals do |

| | | |
|---|---|---|
| hormone | (HOR-mohn) | compounds produced by the endocrine glands that help regulate the activities of the body |
| hypothesis | (hy-POTH-ih-sis) | an idea accepted to be tested by experimental means |
| imprinting | (im-PRIN-ting) | establishment of behavior patterns early on in the life of an organism |
| instincts | (IN-stinktz) | certain behavior patterns that are inborn; example, birds building nests |
| kidneys | (KID-neez) | a pair of organs that remove waste from the blood and make urine |
| kilogram | (KIL-uh-gram) | metric measure that equals 1,000 grams |
| kilometer | (kih-LOM-ih-tur) | metric measure that equals 1,000 meters |
| ligaments | (LIG-uh-munts) | connective tissue that holds bones together |
| linear | (LIN-ee-ur) | measurements of length, width, and height |
| locomotion | (loh-kuh-MOH-shun) | an organism's ability to move through a given environment |
| longevity | (lon-JEV-ih-tee) | span or duration of life |
| marijuana | (mar-uh-HWAN-uh) | a narcotic drug derived from the hemp plant |
| medulla oblongata | (mih-DUL-uh ob-lon-GAH-tuh) | a part of the brain that controls reflex actions such as breathing, sneezing, or swallowing |
| meter | (MEE-tur) | standard unit of length in the metric system equal to 100 cm |
| metric | (MEH-trik) | a system of measurement that is used in most countries and in all scientific work |
| microscopes | (MY-kruh-skohps) | an instrument used to magnify small objects |
| migrate | (MY-grayt) | to move from one place to another; example: birds migrate |
| millimeter | (MIL-uh-mee-tur) | a metric measure equivalent to 1/1,000 of a meter |
| molecules | (MOL-uh-kyoolz) | the smallest part of an element or compound |
| narcotics | (nar-KOT-iks) | addictive drugs |
| naturalist | (NACH-ruh-list) | a person who studies both living and nonliving forms of nature |
| ophthalmologist | (of-thal-MOL-uh-jist) | a doctor (M.D.) who deals with eye disorders |

| | | |
|---|---|---|
| optician | (op-TISH-un) | a person who makes eyeglasses to correct eye defects |
| optometrist | (op-TOM-ih-trist) | a person who prescribes eyeglasses to correct eye defects |
| organisms | (OR-guh-niz-umz) | persons, animals, or plants |
| oxidation | (ok-sih-DAY-shun) | the chemical combination of certain elements with oxygen; oxidation of food produces energy such as heat |
| oxygen | (OK-sih-jun) | colorless, tasteless, odorless element that makes up a fifth of the earth's atmosphere |
| pancreas | (PAN-kree-us) | large digestive gland behind the lower part of the stomach |
| paramecium | (par-uh-MEE-see-um) | a one-celled animal which moves with cilia |
| parasite | (PAR-uh-syt) | an organism that lives on or in another organism and depends on it for nourishment |
| perspiration | (pur-spuh-RAY-shun) | waste excreted through skin pores; sweat |
| pheromone | (FER-uh-mohn) | natural chemical released by insects |
| physics | (FIZ-iks) | the science that deals with matter and energy |
| pituitary | (pih-TOO-ih-ter-ee) | a small ductless gland at the base of the brain that produces many hormones including growth hormones |
| plasma | (PLAZ-muh) | the liquid part of blood which contains cells and dissolved chemicals |
| platelets | (PLAYT-lets) | cells present in the blood that help clotting |
| proteins | (PROH-teenz) | group of organic compounds that contain nitrogen |
| protozoa | (proh-tuh-ZOH-uh) | microscopic one-celled animals |
| psychiatrist | (sy-KY-uh-trist) | a doctor (M.D.) who treats people who are mentally ill |
| psychology | (sy-KOL-uh-jee) | the study of the mind and how it works |
| reflex | (REE-fleks) | an inborn, automatic act performed in response to a stimulus |
| reproduction | (ree-pruh-DUK-shun) | the process by which plants and animals produce others of their kind |
| respiration | (res-puh-RAY-shun) | process of oxidizing food to release energy |
| retina | (RET-uh-nuh) | light-sensitive layer inside the eye |

| | | |
|---|---|---|
| saliva | (suh-LY-vuh) | juice produced by the salivary glands; liquid in the mouth which aids the digestion of starch |
| semicircular canals | (sem-ih-SUR-kyuh-lur) | lymph-filled tubes in the inner ear that control balance |
| spirogyra | (spy-roh-JY-ruh) | pond algae |
| stimulant | (STIM-yuh-lunt) | chemical that arouses activity level; caffeine is a stimulant |
| stomates | (STOH-mayts) | openings on the underside of leaves |
| system | (SIS-tum) | a group of organs that function smoothly in a specialized function; e.g. digestive system |
| tendons | (TEN-dunz) | tissues that connect muscles to bones |
| theory | (THEE-uh-ree) | a set of ideas which offer an accepted explanation of scientific facts and relationships |
| tissue | (TISH-oo) | group of cells that look alike and perform similar functions; muscle cells form muscle tissue |
| transfusion | (trans-FYOO-zhun) | to transfer blood from one person to another |
| translucent | (trans-LOO-sunt) | allows light to go through without being able to see through it |
| tropism | (TROH-piz-um) | a simple response of a plant or animal to a stimulus |
| urinalysis | (yoor-uh-NAL-ih-sis) | a chemical test performed on urine to detect diseases |
| urine | (YOOR-in) | liquid containing body wastes that is released by the kidneys |
| vacuole | (VAK-yoo-ohl) | small space in cell cytoplasm that contains food, wastes, or water |
| volume | (VOL-yoom) | the space taken up by a solid object, a liquid, or a gas |
| vasculum | (VAS-kyuh-lum) | container used to collect fresh plants |
| vagina | (vuh-JY-nuh) | in the female body, the canal leading to the uterus |
| yeast | (YEEST) | colorless plants which reproduce by growing buds |

# Index